The Minor Prophets

James L.R. Catron

Developed as a correspondence course by
Emmaus Correspondence School,
founded in 1942.

Published by:
Emmaus Correspondence School
(A Division of ECS Ministries)
P.O. Box 1028
Dubuque, IA 52004-1028

Cover Design
Ragont Design
Barrington, Illinois

Revised 2005

ISBN 0-940293-53-6

01020304/0908070605

Instructions to Students

The Prophets of the Old Testament addressed the current needs of their day. They spoke out against false prophets, social injustices, rebellion towards God, and meaningless profession. These problems still exist today. In this course the author will help you understand the prophecies of those ancient seers. You will find practical application in the messages of the prophets for your life.

Lessons You Will Study

Introduction
1. The Book of Obadiah—Edom's Doom and Israel's Blessing
2. The Book of Joel—The Day of the Lord
3. The Book of Jonah—God's Will and the Prophet's Service
4. The Book of Amos—The Judgment of God
5. The Book of Hosea—God's Unfailing Love to Israel
6. The Book of Micah—God's Judgment and His Kingdom
7. The Book of Nahum—The Destruction of Nineveh
8. The Book of Zephaniah—God's Judgment and Blessing
9. The Book of Habakkuk—The Perplexities of a Prophet
10. The Book of Haggai—The Rebuilding of the Jewish Temple
11. The Book of Zechariah—Inspiring Israel's Faith and Hope
12. The Book of Malachi—God's Rebuke of Israel's Sin

Course Components

This course has two parts: this textbook and the exam booklet.

The Study Course

The study course contains the lesson material you will use in your studies.

The Exam Booklet

The exam booklet contains all the exams for this course.

How to Study

Begin by asking God to open your heart to receive the truths He would teach you from His Word. Read each chapter through at least twice, once to get the general idea of its contents and then again, slowly, looking up all Scripture references and examining all footnotes. Remember, you may use a dictionary for any terms you do not understand. Do remember to read the relevant chapters from the Bible.

Exams

All the exams are in the Exam Booklet. Before taking each exam, carefully review the relevant chapter material including the Bible references. When you actually come to take the exams, try to do so without reference to the chapter, your Bible or your notebook unless otherwise instructed. The Exam Booklet contains more instructions.

Study Schedule

Begin studying immediately, or if you are in a group, as soon as the group begins. We suggest that you try to complete one chapter each week and take a maximum of one year to finish the course.

How Your Papers Are Graded

Any incorrectly answered questions will be marked by your instructor. You will be referred back to the place in the Bible or the textbook where the correct answer is to be found. You will receive a certificate showing your grade.

Returning Your Exams

See the Exam Booklet for more information on returning your exams.

Introduction to the Minor Prophets

If you are a true believer in Jesus Christ, then you have been given a spiritual gift or gifts. All of God's gifts are sovereignly bestowed. If a man was a prophet in the Old Testament days, it was because God had chosen him to be such, not because of anything in himself which merited this gift. Before we begin our book-by-book studies in the Minor Prophets, it is essential that we learn some general things about prophets and prophecy. The best place to begin is with the word "prophet" itself.

A. THE WORD, PROPHET

1. DEFINITION

The word "prophet" simply means a mouthpiece or spokesman—that is, he was someone who spoke authoritatively for another.

2. ILLUSTRATION (See Exodus 4:16; 7:1-2)

A clear illustration of this meaning of the word "prophet" is found in the book of Exodus where Aaron was commissioned by God to be Moses' prophet (mouthpiece or spokeman). When these two men went in before Pharaoh, Aaron would do all the talking. What he spoke was only what Moses instructed him to say. Aaron was *not the SOURCE* of what was said to Pharaoh, only the instrument (mouthpiece) to convey the message.

3. APPLICATION (See 2 Peter 1:21; Hebrews 1:1)

All the true prophets of God were His spokesmen. They were *not the source* of their own messages, but simply the instruments used of God to convey His Word to the people. Notice that they routinely began their messages, "Thus saith the LORD." The apostle Peter in his second epistle gives a New Testament confirmation of this Old Testament fact: "FOR THE PROPHECY CAME NOT IN OLD TIME BY THE WILL OF MAN: BUT *HOLY MEN OF GOD SPAKE AS THEY WERE MOVED BY THE HOLY GHOST.*"

4. **CLARIFICATION** (See Jeremiah 23:9-40)

Unfortunately, false prophets arose who led the people of God astray. They professed to be true spokesmen for Jehovah but they made up their own messages. Jeremiah has the classic passage in the Old Testament concerning these evil men (23:9-40). Verse sixteen reads, "THUS SAITH THE LORD OF HOSTS, HEARKEN NOT UNTO THE WORDS OF THE PROPHETS (false ones, that is) THAT PROPHESY UNTO YOU: THEY MAKE YOU VAIN: THEY SPEAK A VISION OF THEIR OWN HEART, AND NOT OUT OF THE MOUTH OF THE LORD." But how could one tell the difference between the false and the true representative of Jehovah? There were several tests to determine this:

a. **First, the test of reception** (Deuteronomy 18:9-14)

By what method did the professing prophet of Jehovah receive his message? If he used methods of divination (which God had outlawed), then it was clear that he was not a true spokesman of God and his message was not to be accepted.

b. **Second, the test of fulfillment** (Deuteronomy 18:15-22, especially v. 22)

Did his prophecy come true? Was it fulfilled? If not, then the prophet was proved to be false (see Jeremiah 28).

c. **Third, the test of affirmation** (Deuteronomy 13:1-5)

Did his prophecy affirm or contradict the already known word and will of God. If it contradicted the revealed will of God, then the prophet was proved false and was to be put to death.

Unfortunately, many men (and some women, see Ezekial. 13) became professional prophets for selfish reasons, such as power, prestige and, of course, money. Some were satanically motivated. Even today, there are counterfeits. Paul warned against them in 1 Timothy 6:5, ". . . MEN OF CORRUPT MINDS, AND DESTITUTE OF THE TRUTH, SUPPOSING THAT GAIN IS GODLINESS: FROM SUCH WITHDRAW THYSELF." Or to paraphrase the idea: "who suppose that Christianity is a means of making money."

5. SYNONYMOUS TERMS

The word "prophet" was not the only title of God's spokesman. The Old Testament employs many other terms which give us somewhat of a description of the prophet's character and service. Some of these are:

a. **Seer** (1 Samuel 9:9)

This term emphasizes the subjective side of the prophet's ministry, namely the mode of receiving divine revelation, BY SEEING (note that God is called both a prophet and a seer in 2 Samuel 24:11).

b. **Man of God** (Deuteronomy 33:1, 1 Samuel 9:6; 2 Kings 4:9, etc.)

Moses, Samuel, Elijah and Elisha were all called by this term, which emphasizes their holy calling, character and ministry. In the New Testament, Timothy is called by this term (1 Timothy 6:11).

c. **Servant of the Lord** (1 Kings 14:18; 2 Kings 9:7; 17:13; Jeremiah 7:25; Ezekiel 38:17; Zechariah 1:6)

This title stresses the relationship of the prophet to God. The prophet is not God's equal. He is a servant (compare 1 Corinthians 3:5-8 where Paul identifies with this attitude).

d. **Messenger of the Lord** (Haggai 1:13; Malachi 3:1; 2 Chronicles 36:15-16; Isaiah 44:26)

This title tells us that the prophet's primary work was to deliver God's message to God's people. Note the two categories:

(1) Forth-telling—That is, EXHORTATIVE in nature, telling God's people to get right, and stay right, with Him. Thus, they were first of all divinely appointed moral and ethical preachers.

(2) Fore-telling—That is PREDICTIVE in nature, telling God's people what He has planned for the future.

B. THE MINISTRY OF THE PROPHETS

1. THE CHARACTER OF THEIR MINISTRY

a.   A Ministry of Consecration

These men had a meeting with the living God and it changed them into powerful witnesses for the Lord. This is where all acceptable service for God begins (see especially Isaiah 6).

b.   A Ministry of Identification

They identified with the people of their day. They were not monks or mystics who isolated themselves from the mainstream of life. They made themselves available to the people, moving in and out among them in their everyday life (see Amos, Micah, etc.).

c.   A Ministry of Conviction

They never compromised the truth of God, and they spoke His Word fearlessly. Never could you say of any of them that they were men-pleasers. This is illustrated time and again in their uncompromising rebuke of kings, priests, prophets, and the nobility (see Amos 7, Jeremiah 26, etc.).

d.   A Ministry of Compassion

They spoke out of their hearts. They loved God's people, and though they had some very hard things to communicate, it was all with a view to Israel's preservation and sanctification (see Hosea and Jeremiah as two of the finest examples of prophetic ministry coming from tender hearts).

2. THE COMMUNICATION OF THEIR MINISTRY

These men of God who received their messages through dreams, visions and the audible voice of God used a variety of ways in which to pass on God's message. At times it was just straight-forward preaching (see Amos 1-2), sometimes it was in parables and allegories (see Ezekiel 15, 16), at other times it was through dramatic acting (see Zechariah 11), and several times it was through symbolic action (see 1 Samuel 15:27-31; 1 Kings 11:26-32; Ezekiel 4-5). It should be clear that the method of the communication was dictated by God and not left up to the whim of the prophet (see Hebrews 1:1, "divers manners"). Some of these men were called of God to do things which are not necessarily examples for us to follow. We should seek to follow their example of consecration, identification, conviction, and compassion, but be careful that we do not try to imitate their gift and methods of ministry. We should imitate their godliness and holiness, not their ministry.

3. THE HISTORICAL SETTING OF THEIR MINISTRY

a. **Generally**—Where do the prophets fit into the history of Israel? It would be well for us to briefly sketch the flow of history from the beginning of Israel to the time of the prophets. This will help us keep our sense of historical orientation.

I. THE HISTORY OF MANKIND IN GENERAL .... Genesis 1-11

II. THE HISTORY OF THE CHOSEN COVENANT PEOPLE IN PARTICULAR .... Genesis 12-Malachi

A. PERIOD OF THE PATRIARCHS .... Genesis 12-50
(Abraham, Isaac, Jacob)

B. PERIOD OF THE NATION .... Exodus-Malachi

1. **BEGINNING** OF THE
COVENANT NATION .... Exodus 1-18

2. **CONSTITUTION** OF THE
COVENANT NATION .... Exodus 19-Leviticus 27

3. **ORGANIZATION** OF THE
COVENANT NATION .... Numbers 1-10:10

4. **JOURNEY** OF THE COVENANT NATION
   TO CANAAN .... Numbers 10:11-Deuteronomy 34

5. **LAND-INHERITANCE** OF THE COVENANT
   NATION—CANAAN .... Joshua 1-24

6. **FAILURE** OF THE COVENANT
   NATION (Judges Period). .... Judges-1 Samuel 8

7. **MONARCHY** OF THE
   COVENANT NATION .... 1 Samuel 9-2 Kings 25

8. **EXILE** OF THE COVENANT NATION
   (to Babylon) .... 2 Kings 25 & 2 Chronicles 36
   (see Jeremiah, Daniel & Ezekiel)

9. **RESTORATION** OF THE
   COVENANT NATION
   (from exile) .... Ezra, Nehemiah, Haggai, Zechariah

10. **PRESERVATION** OF THE
    COVENANT NATION .... Esther

Observe that *Esther* depicts life for those Jews who chose to stay in their exile rather than return to Palestine.

b. **Specifically**

Thus, the period of the prophets is from 1 Samuel 9 through the rest of the history of the Old Testament. In other words, from the start of the Monarchy through the Divided Kingdom, the Exile, and the Restoration. There were many, many prophets during this period, but only a few, relatively speaking, left us with a written record of their prophecies (Isaiah through Malachi). These writing prophets, as they are sometimes called, ministered after the division of the kingdom in 931 BC (see chart). The Kingdom was united under Saul, David and Solomon, but became divided into two parts during the reign of Solomon's son, Rehoboam. This story is found in 1 Kings 12 and following. Thus, there came to be a NORTHERN Kingdom which became very idolatrous, and a SOUTHERN Kingdom which continued the line of Daivd. Some of the prophets prophesied in the NORTHERN Kingdom, seeking to call the people back to the worship of the true God, while condemning their evils and warning of coming judgment. Others prophesied in the SOUTHERN Kingdom with a similar message. The NORTHERN Kingdom lasted from 931–722 BC. The Assyrians, as the prophets foretold, became God's chastising instrument to destroy the NORTHERN Kingdom and send its people into captivity. The SOUTHERN Kingdom lasted from 931 to 586 BC when the Babylonians destroyed it, taking its people off to Babylon. The time chart gives the proper orientation as to the centuries in which these men of God prophesied. But how does one determine in which century a prophet lived? The chief way is to note what kings were reigning when the prophet prophesied. This is sometimes given in the superscription (the first verse of a prophetic book. See Hosea 1:1 for example).

1000 BC	900 BC	800 BC	700 BC	600 BC	500 BC

931 BC   722 BC

NORTHERN KINGDOM: Jeroboam - Hoshea

	9th	8th	7th	6th	5th
SAUL DAVID SOL. United King- dom	Obadiah Joel Divided Kingdom	Jonah Amos Hosea Isaiah Micah	Jeremiah . Daniel .... Nahum Habakkuk Zephaniah	. Jeremiah . Daniel Ezekiel Haggai Zechariah	Malachi

SOUTHERN KINGDOM: Rehoboam - Zedekiah

////// Governorships

931 BC............Pre-Exilic Period............605 . Exile . ...539...Post-Exile

LIST OF KINGS AND GOVERNORS OF THE JEWS

	NORTHERN KINGS	SOUTHERN KINGS
10th Century	Jeroboam I ... 931–910 Nadab .... 910–909 Baasha 909–886	Rehoboam ... 931–913 Abijam .... 913–911 Asa 911–870
9th Century	Omri .... 886–874 Ahab .... 874–853 Ahaziah .... 853–852 Joram .... 852–841 Jehu .... 841–814 Jehoahaz 814–798	Jehoshaphat 873–848 Jehoram ...... 853–841 Ahaziah .... 841 Athaliah ...... 841–835 Joash 835–796
8th Century	Jehoash .... 798–782 Jeroboam II .. 793–753* Zechariah ..... 753–752 Shallum .... 752 Pekah .... 752–732 Menahem .... 752–742 Pekahiah ..... 742–740 Hoshea 732–722	Amaziah ...... 796–767 Uzziah .... 790–739 Jotham .... 750–731 Ahaz .... 735–715 Hezekiah 715–686
7th Century		Manasseh .... 695–642 Amon .... 642–640 Josiah .... 640–609 Jehoahaz .... 609 Jehoiakim 609–597
6th Century		Jehoiachin .... 597 Zedekiah 597–586
		EXILE
		Zerubbabel .. 538–??? (governor)
5th Century		Ezra .... 458–??? (governor) Nehemiah .... 445–??? (governor)

*Note that in the dating of the kings there is overlapping for some. This is due to the fact that some of the kings reigned at the same time (father and son). We call these CO–REGENCIES.

PERSIAN KINGS OF THE SIXTH AND FIFTH CENTURIES (539–404 BC)

Cyrus	539–530
Cambyses	530–522
Darius I	522–486
Xerxes	486–464
Artaxerxes I	464–423
Darius II	423–404

1

The Book of Obadiah

Someone has said that "great things often come in small packages." How true that is of Obadiah. Here we have the smallest book in the Old Testament. It is just one chapter of twenty-one verses, but it is a powerful book of holy Scripture. It is going to be very worthwhile for the student to get a firm grasp of this tiny prophecy.

I. THE AUTHOR

A. HIS NAME—Obadiah

This name, Obadiah, means "servant of Jehovah." *Some* of the names of the prophets have prophetic significance—that is, the Lord intended that the meaning of their names have some application to their prophecies. We will note that as we go along in each of the studies. We cannot determine for certain if Obadiah's name has any prophetic significance, but certainly we can say that the prophet sought to live a life consistent with the meaning of his name. We should seek to live consistently with the names we bear: Christians, disciples, etc.

B. HIS IDENTIFICATION—Unknown

We know absolutely nothing of the identity of this prophet. Though the name Obadiah was a popular one in the history of Israel, and though the Old Testament mentions about a dozen different men by this name, there is no sure way of linking this prophet with any of them. Inability to determine the identity does not alter our understanding and appreciation of the book. Besides, since a prophet was only a "mouthpiece," it was his message that was of prime importance, not his person. Some public communicators of God's word have forgotten this; they are attracting people to themselves rather than to the Lord. One proof of a true servant is that he points people to the Lord rather than himself. Someone has said, "If a man is to be remembered for one thing only, what more worthy ground of rememberance can there be than that he was a SERVANT OF THE LORD!"

II. THE BOOK

A. THE THEME OF THE BOOK

The theme of Obadiah is the *Doom of Edom* (1-16) and the *Blessing of Israel* (17-21). In the first part of the theme, the principle of justice by which God operates is stated in verse 15: "AS THOU HAST DONE, IT SHALL BE DONE UNTO THEE: THY REWARD SHALL RETURN UPON THINE OWN HEAD." This is RETRIBUTIVE JUSTICE—that is, Edom will reap what it has sown. Has Edom cut off Israel? Then it will be cut off. Has Edom ransacked Jerusalem? So its rock fortress will be ransacked. Has Edom slaughtered Israel? So it will be slain. The second part of the theme, which is the Blessing of Israel (17-21), is a capsule sketch of what the major prophets (Isaiah, Jeremiah, Ezekiel, Daniel) dwell on in detail. It refers to the future when God will again restore His ancient people. God has promised, unconditionally, to set up his kingdom, and no nation can prevent this.

We can learn some valuable lessons from this two-fold theme: *FIRST,* the apostle Paul warns the Christian, "BE NOT DECEIVED; GOD IS NOT MOCKED: FOR WHATSOEVER A MAN SOWETH, THAT SHALL HE ALSO REAP. FOR HE THAT SOWETH TO HIS FLESH SHALL OF THE FLESH REAP CORRUPTION: BUT HE THAT SOWETH TO THE SPIRIT SHALL OF THE SPIRIT REAP LIFE EVERLASTING" (Galations 6:7-8). How are we sowing?

Edom sowed to the flesh and paid for it! We too will reap what we sow; it is an unchanging Divine law. *SECOND*, the apostle Paul teaches us in 2 Corinthians 1:20, "ALL THE PROMISES OF GOD IN HIM ARE YEA, AND IN HIM AMEN, UNTO THE

GLORY OF GOD." Just as the unconditional promises of God to Israel will be faithfully fulfilled, so all the promises which our Lord has made to the church will find fulfillment. We never have to worry about this, for God is not like us. We are often unfaithful to our promises, but Paul speaks of our God as the "God, that cannot lie . . ." (Titus 1:2), and as the One Who "abideth faithful" (2 Timothy 2:13). This should bring great peace to our hearts.

B. THE READERS

When we write a letter, we begin by addressing the person by name. There is no doubt for whom the letter is intended. But this is not always true of Scripture. For whom was this book originally intended? Was this prophecy sent to Edom to warn them? After all, most of it deals with Edom. We have no record of this. Was it delivered to Israel, since verses 17-21 primarily refer to Israel? We have no record of this either. It would seem that Israel must have been the recipient of this book. God intended it for the comfort and encouragement of His people. The fact that God would judge a nation that hated and hurt Israel, and the fact that He promised to deliver and restore Israel would be a source of hope and comfort. But we are readers of this book too, and God intended that we should gain comfort and hope through the principles found in it. What eternal truths can we find in Obadiah which apply to our personal Christian experience?

C. THE TIME OF WRITING

It can be very frustrating when you receive a letter from a friend and there is no date on it—especially when you refer to it later on and you say, "Now, when did I get this?" This can be a problem with some of the books of Scripture. Obadiah has always been a problem in this regard. No time is referred to in the superscription (1:1) as it is in some of the prophetic books (see Hosea, Amos, etc.). In many of them it is stated in the first chapter and first verse that the prophet prophesied in the reign of a certain king or kings. Since it is easy to determine the time of the kings, it is easy to determine the time of the prophet and his ministry. This is a problem not only for Obadiah, but for Joel, Jonah, Nahum, Habakkuk, and Malachi as well.

Of course, there are other ways to determine the time of the prophet and his writing besides the use of the superscription. Sometimes there are time-references within the prophet's book, and sometimes the prophet is referred to in some other book of Scripture. For instance, though no specific time is mentioned in Jonah, we know that Jonah prophesied in the eighth century B.C. because he is mentioned in 2 Kings 14:25 in regard to the reign of Jeroboam II, an eighth century king of the Northern Kingdom.

But what about Obadiah? Is there some time reference within his book which can help to place him? Yes, there is. Verses 10-14 speak of an invasion of Jerusalem in which much spoil was taken, many were slain, captives were taken, and EDOM WAS AN ALLY IN THIS INVASION. Now when did this happen? If we can determine this, then we can find a date for the writing of Obadiah. The Old Testament reveals that Jerusalem was invaded four times. See the chart:

BY SHISHAK OF EGYPT—926	BY THE PHILISTINES, ARABIANS AND EDOM IN 845	BY JEHOASH OF THE NORTHERN KINGDOM—790	BY BABYLON IN 586
1 Kings 14:25,26 2 Chronicles 12	2 Chronicles 21:16,17 2 Kings 8:20-22	2 Kings 14 2 Chronicles 25	2 Kings 25 2 Chronicles 36
#1	#2	#3	#4

Numbers 1 and 3 are out of the question; numbers 2 and 4 are possibilities. Number 2 seems to be the most likely date; this was during the reign of Jehoram of Judah (848-841). Edom had revolted against Judah during the reign of Jehoram and was a bitter enemy of Judah at this time (see 2 Kings 8:20-22; 2 Chronicles 21:8-20). The invasion of 586 seems to go beyond what Obadiah describes. Obadiah does not mention the deportation of all of Judah and Jerusalem as happened in number 4. A ninth century date for the prophet seems more consistent with Obadiah. For a full discussion of this see A SURVEY OF OLD TESTAMENT INTRODUCTION, by Gleason Archer, pages 287–289, published by Moody Press.

D. THE BACKGROUND OF THE BOOK

The book of Obadiah opens with "Thus saith the Lord God concerning Edom . . ." Who is Edom? Where was Edom located? How did Edom's history develop? It is very important to ponder these questions because the answers to them help us to understand the meaning of the book.

1. WHO IS EDOM?—"Esau is Edom . . ." Genesis 36:8

The book of Obadiah concerns the descendants of two men who were the children of Isaac and Rebekah—ESAU and JACOB. The Edomites descended from Esau who was Jacob's twin, and the Israelites descended from Jacob. The story of their birth is recorded in Genesis 25:19-26 where we are told that Isaac prayed that God would provide his barren wife with a child. God answered by providing twins. Esau is considered the elder of the two because he came out of the womb first. God decreed that two nations would come from these two boys and that the "one people shall be stronger than the other people; and *the elder shall serve the younger.*" This is exactly how things worked out, as the Old Testament repeatedly affirms (see Malachi 1:2-4). Esau hated Jacob bitterly (read Genesis 27) and wanted to kill him, but Rebekah intervened (27:42-45) by sending Jacob away to Padan-aram. Years later there was a reconciliation between the two brothers when Jacob returned from Padan-aram (Genesis 33:1-16), but this was shown to be superficial by the continuing hatred that Esau's descendants had for Israel. Throughout the history of these two peoples, Edom constantly showed a spirit of hateful revenge. Learn a lesson from this as regards your personal relationship with others in the family of God. Always keep the lines of communication open. If believers have conflicts with one another, these should be resolved immediately lest they get out of hand and affect the whole body of believers. Hate and revenge are destructive and the first to be destroyed are those who harbor these sins.

2. WHERE WAS EDOM LOCATED? See Maps

Of course, we know that Jacob's descendants were given the promised land, "a land flowing with milk and honey." But what about Esau and his posterity? If we had a choice of where we wanted to live, we would never have chosen Esau's territory. Esau did not have a choice, for God appointed to him his land portion. Isaac, speaking for God made the initial statement concerning the future location of Edom: "BEHOLD, AWAY FROM THE FERTILITY OF THE EARTH SHALL BE YOUR DWELLING, AND AWAY FROM THE DEW OF HEAVEN FROM ABOVE" (NASV, Genesis 27:39)— that is, it will be the opposite of the fertile land of promise given to Israel. But where, geographically? The book of Deuteronomy gives the answer: ". . . I HAVE GIVEN MT. SEIR TO ESAU AS A POSSESSION . . . THE HORITES FORMERLY LIVED IN SEIR. BUT THE SONS OF ESAU

Maps Showing the Location of Edom

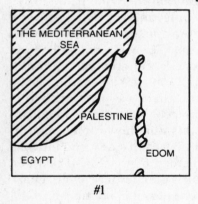

#1

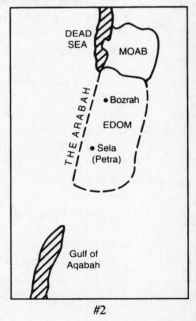

#2

DISPOSSESSED THEM AND DESTROYED THEM
FROM BEFORE THEM AND SETTLED IN THEIR
PLACE" (2:5, 12). Mt. Seir fits well the description of Isaac:
"AWAY FROM the fertility of the earth . . . AWAY FROM
the dew of heaven . . ." Mt. Seir is the range of mountains
running southward from the Dead Sea just east of the valley
of Arabah. In this rugged, mountainous area is a rock fortress
called Sela (Petra) which was the capital city of ancient Edom.
The Edomites felt that no one could conquer them in their
city of security, but God said, "I WILL BRING THEE DOWN
. . ." (Obadiah 4). No one can escape the judgment of God!
It is far better to trust in the living God than in the battle-
ments of men.

3. HOW DID EDOM'S HISTORY DEVELOP?

Quite a bit of time elapses between the history of Esau, the father
of the Edomites, in Genesis and the first mention of the nation
which came from him. The next we hear of Esau's descendants is
in the books of Numbers and Deuteronomy. The first contact
between Israel and Edom comes in Numbers 20:14-21 as Israel
is traveling toward the promised land. Israel asks permission to
pass through Edomite territory but is refused. This is a key passage, showing that Esau's hatred of Jacob is continued in his posterity. Hundreds of years pass, and David (in fulfillment of Genesis
27:40a and Numbers 24:17-18) brings Edom into subjection.
However, Edom later asserts itself and breaks the yoke of complete subjection to Israel (see 2 Kings 8:20-22). When Babylon
was a strong power, Edom came under its yoke and was warned
along with others not to rebel (Jeremiah 27:1-11). By the time of
the prophet Malachi, the Edomites had already been driven from
Mt. Seir by the confederates they trusted (Obadiah 1:7 and
Malachi 1:3-5). Some Edomites settled in Southern Judah (called
Idumea) in and around Hebron. Later, around 125 BC, in the
period between the Old and New Testaments, John Hyrcanus, a
second generation Maccabee, made the Edomites become Jews.
Josephus, the Jewish historian, records: "Hyrcanus also took Dora
and Merissa, cities of Idumea, and subdued all the Idumeans;
and permitted them to stay in that country, IF THEY WOULD

SUBMIT TO CIRCUMCISION, AND MAKE USE OF THE
LAWS OF THE JEWS . . ." (Book XIII, Chapter IX). The last
we hear of the Edomites is 70 AD when Jerusalem was destroyed
by the Romans.

OUTLINE OF THE BOOK OF OBADIAH

The outline of Obadiah is based on the themes, *The Doom of Edom*
(1-16), and *The Blessing of Israel* (17-21).

1. **THE DOOM OF EDOM** 1-16

    a. The **PREDICTION** of the Doom of Edom 1-2

    Obadiah's prediction of the coming doom of Edom is not due to
    any exceptional human foresight on his part as he reflects on the
    political and religious conditions of the day. What he proclaims is
    "THUS SAITH THE LORD." Edom's sin is great and Obadiah
    declares that God will make it "small among the heathen," or as
    someone has put it, "cut it down to size!" How does God see us?

    b. The **CERTAINTY** of the doom of Edom 3-4

    Edom followed Satan's sin: "The pride (arrogance) of thine heart
    hath deceived thee." The deception was so great that they believed
    no one could destroy them. Their trust was in their well-fortified
    and well-located rock fortress. But Edom did not take God into
    consideration. Arrogance never does! So God says, "I will bring
    thee down." Remember, "Pride goeth before destruction, and a
    haughty spirit before a fall" (Proverbs 16:18; see also 26:12; 29:23;
    Isaiah 2:12). The way up is the way down (1 Peter 5:6).

    c. The **COMPLETENESS** of the Doom 5-6

    When God's judgment strikes, it will not be just a casual raid by
    a band of thieves. A casual raid would not devastate the place.
    Edom is to be utterly ruined and plundered. Arrogance is always
    the loser! Blessed are the poor in spirit!

d. The **INSTRUMENTS** of the Doom of Edom 7

Edom trusted not only its rock fortress, but also its allies. This was its undoing. For God turned them against Edom. "All the men of thy confederacy . . . the men that were at peace with thee have deceived thee, and prevailed against thee; . . ." This verse tells us the means that God used to judge Edom. This divine method is illustrated many times over in Scripture.

e. The **RESULTS** of the Doom of Edom 8-9

The wise men whose arrogant policies guided the nation of Edom, and the army ("mighty men") who guarded the nations would be destroyed. This is the only fitting result for arrogance. It must be destroyed.

f. The **REASON** for the Doom of Edom 10-14

The pride of Edom's *heart* was manifested in Edom's *deeds*. What you think of others is evidenced in how you act toward them. Edom had a hateful spirit of revenge toward his brother, Israel. These verses tell of a time when Edom participated in a cruel invasion of Jerusalem and acted in a very unbrotherly, inhuman way. Edom did not consider him to be his "brother's keeper." How do we treat our brothers and sisters? Hebrews 13:1 says, "Let brotherly love continue," and in 1 John 3:15 we are warned that "Whosoever hateth his brother is a murderer . . ."

g. The **JUSTICE** of the Doom of Edom 15-16

The justice of the doom of Edom is based on the principle of sowing and reaping. "As you have done, it will be done to you." Edom will simply reap what it has sown! This applies to us as well, because God has not changed this law. Let us be careful what we sow.

It should be noted that these verses bring before us a cardinal principle of Old Testament prophecy—namely, "the universal prediction growing out of the local circumstances." So Obadiah speaks of "the day of the Lord is near upon *all the heathen (nations): . . .*"

The judgment upon Edom becomes a picture or illustration of the judgment of God upon all nations in the "day of the Lord." The nations of the future "day of the Lord" will reap what they have sown (Matthew 25:31-46). The Old Testament prophets speak in this two-fold manner many, many times.

2. THE BLESSING OF ISRAEL 17-21

The prophet Obadiah now passes to the second and the brighter part of his picture—the future blessing of Israel.

a. The Blessing of **DELIVERANCE** 17

In the future "day of the Lord" Israel will experience deliverance in the Holy Land—Mt. Zion being specifically pointed out here.

b. The Blessing of **TRIUMPH** 18

Under the leadership of God Israel will participate in the coming deliverance spoken of in verse seventeen. They will be victors, and Edom (as well as all nations, verses 15, 16) will be the vanquished. The prophet Zechariah speaks at greater length concerning this (Zechariah 12-14). Keep in mind that though Edom passed off the scene after 70 AD, it, like other nations, will be revived in the future "day of the Lord." Some passages that infer that Edom will indeed be involved in the future tribulation are: Daniel 11:41; Joel 3:18-21; Amos 9:11-15.

c. The Blessing of **RE-POSSESSING THE LAND** 19-20

The thought here is that of exiles returning to their homeland. You will remember that, hundreds of years before, Joshua had brought the people of Israel into Canaan to the land which God had promised them. That was in 1405 BC. Israel never did occupy the land fully. In a coming day, when God brings his people from afar, they will POSSESS it. Ezekiel says, "YES, I WILL CAUSE MEN—MY PEOPLE ISRAEL—TO WALK ON YOU AND POSSESS YOU SO THAT YOU WILL BECOME THEIR INHERITANCE AND NEVER AGAIN BEREAVE THEM O CHILDREN" (Ezekiel 36:12). These verses (19, 20) are just a *sample picture* of the fulfillment of the promise of the land made to Abraham in Genesis 12, 13, 15, etc.

What a wonderful note on which to end this brief prophecy: "... AND THE KINGDOM SHALL BE THE LORD'S." The first Adam, because of sin, lost the dominion which God had given to him and his posterity (compare Genesis 1:26 with Genesis 3 and Hebrews 2:6-8). The last Adam, Jesus Christ, will regain this dominion for man, for God has decreed it (compare Psalm 2:6-9 with Revelations 11:15). But the way to victory over sin and Satan had to be by way of the cross. There could be no kingdom without the cross! Jesus must die the awful death of the cross! And He did! Praise God, JESUS SHALL REIGN!

SUMMARY

Edom is despised and God will make it small among the nations. Its rock fortress will not be a safe refuge from God, and it will be completely ravaged. Ironically, Edom's allies will turn against it and the result will be that its vaunted wisdom and military might well be destroyed. Edom is simply reaping what it has sown and thus God is just in judging it. What Edom experiences will be the lot of all nations in the "day of the Lord." In contrast, Israel will be greatly blessed of God: delivered from domination and oppression, triumphing over its ancient enemies—especially revived Edom (in the context), having its land restored to it, and coming under the reign of God. God is going to have the last word in the history of man. Jesus shall reign! Is He King of *your* life now?

2

The Book of Joel

Tragic things happen every day, and when we hear of disasters in our land and throughout the world, our hearts immediately go out to those who are torn by great suffering—from earthquakes, floods, famine, disease, and, of course, war. The "why" of specific suffering is not always revealed to us, but the Bible does teach that suffering is sometimes allowed by God as a means of maturing us in our faith (see Job, James 1:2-4; Romams 5:3-4). The Bible also makes it quite clear that God sometimes uses tragedy as a chastising instrument because of sin in our lives. The whole book of Lamentation is an eloquent illustration of this, as is the first part of the book which we have before us in this study.

"What a tragic hour it was for God's ancient people. The nation was experiencing an invasion of locusts (1:4-13). God had revealed to Israel through Moses that if His people persisted in sin, He would use several means to bring them back to Himself. If these did not work, then He would uproot them from their land and drive them into captivity (Deuteronomy 28). So the Lord had brought locusts, just as he had warned in Deuteronomy 28:38-42. Thousands upon thousands of these insects had come in wave after wave, destroying everything in their path. Besides this, a very serious drought had come upon them to complete the picture of tragedy. Desperation pervades the scene and there was only one way to turn—back to God!" (G. Shunk).

We feel sorry for these suffering people, but sin persisted in is not easily abandoned unless God deals severely with us. Let us not think ill of God by despising the chastening of the Lord. He chastens because he loves us, though "no chastening for the present seemeth to be joyous, but grievous" (Hebrews 12:5-15). So God raised up the prophet Joel to call upon His people to lament, to fast, and to repent. Who is this dynamic preacher of the prophetic message?

I. THE AUTHOR

A. HIS NAME

The name Joel occurs often in the Old Testament, there being about a dozen men who bore it. It means YAHWEH is God. YAHWEH (or as some have transliterated it, JEHOVAH) is the personal name of the God of Israel. As with Obadiah, we are not sure if Joel's name has any prophetic significance, or whether it was merely given by his parents as a reflection of their own faith and godliness. If Joel prophesied, as some scholars believe, at a time when Baal worship was strong in Judah, then the very meaning of his name would be a strong rebuke to those who were involved in idolatry. It is clear from his prophecy where Joel's allegiance and loyalty lay, and so in this sense his life was a shining example of the name his parents gave him. What is our confession? Is it, "JESUS IS LORD?" If so, then may our lives match this testimony of our lips.

B. HIS IDENTIFICATION

Our curious minds will not be fully satisfied on this point. The only thing we know about his personal background is given in 1:1 where he is spoken of as the son of Pethuel. Just as in the case of Obadiah, God has not considered it necessary for us to have a biographical sketch of his life. Obscurity in this case is the will of God. Once again, it is the message that is of prime importance, not the prophet. May we be humble, willing servants of our Lord, not concerned about our position and reputation in God's service, but concerned solely for the glory of God.

II. THE BOOK

A. THE THEME OF THE BOOK

Have you noticed in reading Joel that there is a recurring expression of great importance? It is *"the day of the Lord."* Several times over this term is used (1:15; 2:1,11,31; 3:14). Other prophets use the term, too—in fact, you will remember that it was used in Obadiah 15. Sometimes this term is described as "that day," "that great and terrible day." See, for instance, the book of Zephaniah for a variety of ways in which it is described.

Now, the theme of the book of Joel is *"THE DAY OF THE LORD."* What does this mean? The term is used primarily in the Old Testament of God's judgment (Isaiah 2:12; 10:20; 13:6, 9; Ezekiel 13:5; 30:3; Amos 5:18-20; Zephaniah 1:7-15; Zechariah 14:1 and there are many more). It is not necessarily to be understood just as a twenty-four hour day, but as a period of time. The Old Testament uses it to refer to judgments which God brought on His people in ancient days, and it is used of a yet-future day of judgment in the end-times. Joel uses it both ways, and that is how the theme of Joel is developed. The book is divided into two major sections (see outline). The first section uses the term "day of the Lord" of God's judgment in Joel's day *upon the Southern Kingdom* (1:15; 2:1, 11). The second section uses it of God's end-time judgment upon the whole world (2:31; 3:14).

We must be clear that this term is not used of the New Testament church. The church will have been caught up into God's presence before this day of judgment takes place on earth (1 Thessalonnians 4:13-5:9; 2 Thessalonians 2:1-3; Revelation 3:10). God has not appointed the church to the wrath of the tribulation period. The church will not be on earth during this time. However, when the church is taken up to heaven, each believer will stand before the judgment seat of Christ. This is not a time of punishment but of evaluation with a view to reward. How will we fare in that day? Will it be simply, "Saved; yet so as by fire" (1 Corinthians 3:15), or will it be a grand day of reward for the faithful, loving service rendered to the One who loved us and gave Himself for us (2 Corinthians 5:10; 1 Corinthians 3:13, 14)? "ONLY ONE LIFE, TWILL SOON BE PAST, ONLY WHAT'S DONE FOR CHRIST WILL LAST!"

B. THE RECIPIENTS OF THIS PROPHECY

For whom was this prophetic message intended? There is no doubt that it was delivered to the Southern Kingdom—especially Jerusalem. A general reading of the book will demonstrate this because Mt. Zion (2:1,15) is mentioned, and the priests and temple (1:13; 2:17) are a part of the setting. Joel probably lived in Jerusalem. Thus, the Southern Kingdom has corrupted itself by some terrible sin (Joel doesn't identify it) and God is severely punishing it (1:1-20). The Southern Kingdom was the last stronghold of the true faith. Unlike the Northern Kingdom, the

Southern Kingdom sought to maintain the pure worship of Jehovah. What has happened? What sin has emerged that merits such strong, punitive measures? Perhaps this can be answered under our discussion of the next point which is the "Time of Communicating the Message." When did Joel deliver this prophecy?

C. THE TIME OF COMMUNICATING THE MESSAGE

No time-element is mentioned in the superscription of Joel (1:1) telling us when he prophesied. However, there are time-references within the book which point to Joel's being a pre-exilic prophet. For instance, the enemies mentioned in chapter 3 (Phoenicians, Philistines, Egyptians, Edomites) were the early enemies of Judah. Then, the book gives the impression that during the time of Joel, Jerusalem was under the control of the priests (royalty is not mentioned in the book). "Was there a time in the history of Judah in pre-exilic times when Judah and Jerusalem were under the control of the priests? Yes, without doubt. The background for this is found in the Kings and Chronicles (2 Kings 11; 2 Chronicles 23-24) when the boy-king, Joash, was not old enough to rule on his own. The nation for all practical purposes was under the direction of Jehoiada, the High Priest, who was the guardian of Joash, the regent until the time that he could rule on his own. This was about 835 BC and so it would be the ninth century."

Here's what happened: "Queen Athaliah, a wicked Baal worshipper, and daughter of Queen Jezebel of the Northern Kingdom, had taken over the Southern Kingdom when her son, King Ahaziah, died. She was a usurper and tried to exterminate the royal line of Judah. In the providence of God, little Joash, one of the royal children, escaped her slaughter and was hidden by the High Priest, Jehoiada, for some six years. A plan was concocted whereby the boy Joash was crowned king and wicked Queen Athaliah was removed. But Athaliah and her son, King Ahaziah, had corrupted the Southern Kingdom by introducing and promoting Baal worship" (G. Shunk).

Again, we ask the question, what sin was the nation involved in that merited such a disastrous punishment as described in Joel, chapter one? The answer is simple: It was BAAL WORSHIP.

We should remember that our God is a Jealous God and He will not stand by indifferently while we give our loyalty to the idols of this world. John warned in his first epistle: "Little children, keep yourselves from idols" (1 John 5:21). Our idols may not be made of wood or stone, but idolatry is not limited to these. Remember that Paul taught that "covetousness" is idolatry (Colossians 3:5). Whatever comes between ourselves and God is an idol. To persist in disloyalty is to invite the fatherly chastening of our God. He loves us too much to allow us to destroy ourselves (Revelation 3:19).

OUTLINE OF THE BOOK OF JOEL

You will recall that Joel's theme is "THE DAY OF THE LORD," a time of judgment. In Joel, this theme has reference both to the day and age of Joel (1:1-2:27) and to a yet future day of tribulation coming upon the whole earth (2:28-3:21).

1. THE DAY OF THE LORD, PAST 1:1-2:27

The first section of Joel has to do with Joel's lifetime. An invasion of literal locusts has come upon the land of Judah.

a. The Servant Who Announces the Locust Invasion 1:1

We already know who this is. It is Joel, the son of Pethuel. See previous comments on his identity.

b. The Comparison of the Locust Invasion 1:2,3

This is a judgment which is worse than any locust invasion Judah has ever experienced, and the story of it is to be passed on to succeeding generations. Why? Because God expects history to be a tool in teaching us not to repeat the mistakes of the past. If we do not learn from history, we can expect to suffer from the same mistakes.

c. The Severity of the Locust Invasion 1:4-18

The whole land is made desolate by wave after wave of these destroying insects. Agriculture is ruined (vines, trees, grain, etc.), and every person is affected. The challenge goes out to "awake . . .

weep . . . wail . . . lament . . . be ashamed . . . gird yourselves and lament . . . sanctify a fast, call a solemn assembly . . . cry unto the Lord." It is an hour of awful desolation! It is the "day of the Lord" (1:15; 2:1). Keep in mind *all the time* that this is not just an unusual act of nature, but God's doing. This invasion of locusts is called "His army" (2:11), and "My great army which I sent among you" (2:25).

d. The Supplication in the Midst of the Locust Invasion 1:19-20

Joel is not only a mighty preacher and exhorter, but a man of prayer. He is in anguish over the desolation. It is in this prayer that we learn that along with the locust invasion there is a drought ("rivers of water are dried up"). I am sure that Joel prayed at other times than in adverse situations, but it is sorrowful indeed, and tragic, that some of God's people only pray when they have their backs to the wall. Let us determine to "pray without ceasing" (1 Thessalonians 5:17).

e. The Description of the Locust Invasion 2:1-11

The *call to alarm* is repeated (compare 2:1a with 1:14), and the locust invasion ("day of the Lord") is described. A locust invasion can consist of literally billions of locusts. "The language of verse two, though vivid, is not exaggerated. Those who have observed such an attack of locusts say that the clouds, darkness and gloom of verse two are literally true" (J. Graybill).

The National Geographic Magazine (Volume XXVIII) December, 1915, contains the description of a severe locust plague which occurred in Jerusalem in 1915. G. A. Smith says: "No one who has seen a cloud of locusts can question the realism even of this picture; the heavy gloom of the immeasurable mass of them, shot by gleams of light where a few of the sun's imprisoned beams have broken through or across the storm of lustrous wings. This is like dawn beaten down upon the hilltops, and crushed by rolling masses of cloud, in conspiracy to prolong the night."

It should be observed that some take this account of a locust invasion as a picture of a yet future invasion of an army of people at the end of the tribulation period—at the battle of Armageddon. There is no doubt that the Bible teaches there will be such a future battle, but is seems better to consider this simply as a locust invasion, for several reasons. Note just two: (1) If you study carefully 2:1-11 you will observe that it is a locust invasion compared to a human army, *NOT* a human army compared to a locust invasion. (2) The locusts are called "His army," and "My great army" (see 2:11 and 2:25).

f. The Exhortation in View of the Locust Invasion ... 2:11-17

The desolation of the locust invasion can be stopped and the locust army removed. But how? Joel, the preacher, gives the divine answer to their dilemma. It is REPENTANCE! They must repent and turn to the Lord. *When* should they repent? "Yet even now" (2:12a NASV). How should they repent? "With all your HEART . . . rend your heart . . . fasting, weeping, mourning . . ." (2:12b-13a NASV). *Why* should they repent? "For He is gracious and compassionate . . . and relenting of the evil . . ." (2:13b-14 NASV). *Where* should they repent? "Blow a trumpet in Zion . . ." (2:15 NASV). *Who* should repent? "People . . . elders . . . children . . . priest . . ." (2:16, 17 NASV). *What* will happen if they repent? "Then the Lord will be zealous for His land, and will have pity on His people . . ." This last question is really the subject of the next point (2:18 NASV).

g. The Promise of Relief from the Locust Invasion 2:18-27

The promise of relief, as we have seen, is based on the repentance of the people of Judah. If they repent, they can expect the removal of the locust invasion, a removal of the drought by the return of the early and later rains, the restoration of "the years that the locust hath eaten, etc." It should be noted that some translations render verse eighteen in the past tense. This would tell us that the people did repent. Are you seeing God's blessing in your life? If not, is there something you need to turn away from in repentance? Do it today, right now! God loves to bless His people!

2. THE DAY OF THE LORD, YET-FUTURE 2:28-3:21

With verse 28, we leap over the centuries to a time which is yet-future to us, living in this day of grace. We go from a *past, local* situation to a *yet-future, universal* situation. In the future judgment of God in "the day of the Lord" God's judgment will be on the nations, but His blessing will be seen in the giving of His Spirit and the deliverance of His people so that they might experience the blessings of His kingdom on earth.

a. The Pouring Out of the Holy Spirit 2:28, 29

God will pour out His Holy Spirit in abundance upon all mankind. There will be no barriers of race, sex, age, or class. This outpouring will be accompanied by certain signs of the Holy Spirit's presence (prophesying, dreams, visions, etc.). Pentecost (Acts 2) was an *illustration* of this great outpouring which will be *completely fulfilled* in the tribulation period. Merrill Unger in his "New Testament Teaching on Tongues" (pp. 25, 26) confirms this viewpoint:

> "The specific reason why Peter introduced his Pentecostal sermon with a long quotation from Joel's prophecy (2:17-21) was to show his multilingual Jewish listeners, gathered from all parts of the Roman Empire to celebrate the Feast of Pentecost, that the strange exhibition of languages by the simple Galilean followers of Jesus was not an instance of drunkenness or emotional excess. On the contrary, it was something paralleled by their own prophetic Scriptures, closely akin to similar spiritual phenomena predicted to be visited upon their own race previous to establishment in kingdom blessing.

> It is quite obvious that Peter did not quote Joel's prophecy in the sense of its fulfillment in the events of Pentecost, but purely as a *prophetic illustration of those events.* As a matter of fact, to avoid confusion Peter's quotation evidently purposely goes beyond any possible fulfillment at Pentecost by including events in the still-future day of the Lord, preceding kingdom establishment (Acts 2:19, 20).

> "Peter's phraseology "THIS IS THAT" means nothing more than that "THIS IS (an illustration of) THAT WHICH WAS SPOKEN BY THE PROPHET JOEL" (Acts 2:16). In the reference there is not the slightest hint at a continued fulfillment during the church age or a coming fulfillment toward the end of the church age. *The reference is solely in an illustrative sense* to Jewish listeners at Pentecost. Fulfillment of

Joel's prophecy is still future and awaits Christ's second coming in glory and a copious spiritual outpouring ushering in kingdom blessing (cf. Zechariah 12:10–13:1; Acts 1:6,7)."

Those who believe in the Lord Jesus in this age of grace are given the Holy Spirit immediately (Ephesians 1:13).

b. The Prediction of Signs 2:30, 31

The signs are catastrophes in both earth and heaven. They are presented very generally here, and they denote God's intervention in the affairs of men. These general references are expanded in detail in Rev. 6-19. The church will not be on earth at this time.

c. The Promise of Deliverance 2:32

Deliverance is for "*whosoever*" and the condition is simply "whosoever shall *call* on the name of the Lord." To call implies repentance and faith. Paul uses part of this verse in Romans 10:13. The promise is for now as well as later. Have you taken advantage of it? If not, why don't you trust Christ as your Savior now! He died for you that you might be delivered from sin and judgment.

d. The Proclamation of Judgment upon the Nations 3:1-17

After the Church is caught up to heaven, there will be the events of the tribulation period (Daniel's 70th week, Daniel 9). The tribulation period will close with the literal second coming of Christ to earth. When He comes, He will judge the nations. This is referred to in Matthew 25:31-46. This second chapter of Joel gives us some aspects of this judgment:

(1) The Time of It—"in those days, and in that time" 3:1

This will be at the end-time when God restores the fortunes of Israel.

(2) The Subjects of It—"gather all nations" (3:2a, cf. Matthew. 25)

(3) The Place of It—"and will bring them down into the valley of Jehoshaphat" (3:2b)

This valley is unidentifiable today. One tradition is that it is the Kidron valley. Some feel that we have here a play of words. *Jehoshaphat* means judgment, so all Joel is saying is that God will bring the nations into the valley of judgment.

(4) The Reason for It—"for my people and for my heritage Israel, whom they have scattered among the nations, and parted my land" (3:2c-3)

The reason is the ill-treatment which the nations have given Israel over the centuries. Joel draws into focus the nations who were the early enemies of Israel as illustrations of ill-treatment. (3:4-8)

(5) The Call to It—"Proclaim ye this among the Gentiles; Prepare war, wake up the mighty men, let all the men of war draw near; let them come up;" (3:9-14).

In this section the prophet Joel is emotionally taken up with what the Lord is going to do. In a sense, he is crying out, "Let's get on with it!" Joel wants the Lord to be vindicated by His intervention in the affairs of men. "Let's get on with it! Pour out your anger upon the nations of the earth because of their wickedness and ungodliness!" This refers to the time of Armageddon. "But this battle will take a strange turn. God's mighty ones—the heavenly armies—will come down to fight (v. 11, c.f. Revelation 19:14), and God will sit to judge the nations as when one puts the sickle to the ripe grain (Matthew 13:39), or treads the grapes in the wine press (v. 13; Isaiah 63:1-6; Revelations 14:14-20)" (J. Graybill).

(6) The Terrifying Character of It—(3:15, 16a) The terrifying character of that day is emphasized when the sun and the moon are darkened (15), God roars like a lion (Amos 1:2; Jeremiah 25:30), and the universe shakes (16). This is the "great day of the Lord," of which the locust invasion of 1–2:27 was but a faint forecast.

(7) **The Preservation from It**—(3:16b-17)

Yet the same God who is the *terror* of the nations is the *hope* of His people. They will be defended. All Israel will know certainly that God is dwelling with His people in Jerusalem, which will be forever cleansed from the defilement of the Gentiles.

e. **The Prospects of Millennial Kingdom Blessing** 3:18-21

The second coming of Christ does not bring time to an end. Christ will reign over the earth for 1,000 years. Rejected at His first coming, He will be vindicated in His coming reign. There are many prophecies concerning this millennial reign. Joel concludes his prophecy on the triumphant note of Israel's prosperity and exaltation. The reason for this coming blessing is in the last phrase of verse 21: "FOR THE LORD DWELLETH IN ZION!" As with the last verse of Obadiah, JESUS SHALL REIGN! Is He reigning as King in your life now?

By way of clarification, it should be noted that many from the nations will be saved in that last day. Matthew 25 speaks of the "sheep nations" on Christ's right hand. These will go into the Kingdom because they had responded to the call of the gospel and believed on the Lord Jesus Christ.

CHAPTER

3

The Book of Jonah

Who hasn't heard of Jonah? Who hasn't heard of the great fish that swallowed him up? Who hasn't heard how Jonah miraculously survived his time in the belly of the fish, how three days later he was vomited up on dry land, thereafter to travel to the city of Nineveh and preach a message of judgment that was the means of converting the whole city to the Lord! What a fantastic book this is! It is filled with the miraculous power of God! Jonah is the best known of all the Minor Prophets. Why is that the case? Why is it that you know more about the story of Jonah than you do of all the other Minor Prophets? The answer is simple: it is because it is a *story about the man,* Jonah, rather than a record of his prophecies. It is easy for us to remember stories about famous people who have done great exploits. God wants us to learn about this man because He knows that in so doing we will learn about ourselves. We are all like Jonah in some ways and at some time in our lives. Another reason we know so much about Jonah is that the book is written in simple story-form prose rather than poetry (chapter two is an exception to this, for it is a psalm written in the style of the book of Psalms). Of course, we want to know *more* about Jonah, and we want to see how we can benefit from his story in our Christian lives. Let's begin with Jonah, the man.

I. THE AUTHOR

A. HIS NAME

Jonah's name means "dove." The dove is a symbol of *peace.* Someone has humorously commented that Jonah, in his personality, seems to be more of a hawk than a dove because he didn't want God to spare ancient Nineveh from the judgment he had preached.

God wanted Jonah to be a messenger of "peace" to the Ninevites, but peace could only come as they were challenged with a message of judgement—"yet forty days and Nineveh shall be overthrown." This was meant to bring them to repentance and faith. Possibly, then, it was the divine will that the meaning of his name (dove = peace) should have evangelistic significance in connection with the greatest task that God had ever called Jonah to accomplish— the conversion of an entire city, Nineveh. You may never be used like Jonah, but you can communicate the message of peace which is found in the gospel (Colossians 1:20; Acts 10:36; Romans 5:1).

B. HIS BACKGROUND

We know more about Jonah than about Obadiah and Joel, because Jonah is mentioned not only in his book but in 2 Kings 14:23-25. What can we learn about Jonah's background?

First, his father's name is Amittai (Jonah 1:1; 2 Kings 14:25). We don't know anything about his father other than his name.

Second, he prophesied during the reign of Jeroboam II who reigned in the Northern Kingdom from 793–753 BC. Jonah prophesied some military success for this wicked king (2 Kings 14:25).

Third, we learn that he was from the town of *Gath-hepher.* This was a town in the tribal area of Zebulon, and as you can see by the map, it was near the sea of Galilee (2 Kings 14:25). Gath-hepher was about three miles from Nazareth where several centuries later Jesus grew up into manhood. Some other prophets ministered in Northern Palestine (Hosea, Amos), but the greatest of them all was Jesus who said in Matthew 12:41: "a greater than Jonah is here."

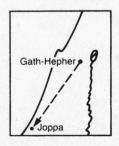

Fourth, we learn in comparing Jonah 1:17 with Matthew 12:40 that Jonah was a type of our Lord Jesus Christ in His burial and resurrection. "As Jonah was three days and three nights in the whale's belly; so shall the Son of man be three days and three nights in the heart of the earth."

Fifth, we learn in comparing Jonah 3 with Luke 11:29-30 that Jonah was a sign, *himself,* to the Ninevites. Evidently they knew of his experience in the great fish and this reinforced his message of judgment.

II. THE BOOK

A. THE THEME OF THE BOOK OF JONAH

The theme of Jonah is Jonah himself, in relation to the will of God in his service as a prophet. God is pre-eminently interested in the maturing and development of His children. He knows that, when we first come to faith and begin to serve Him, there are rough edges which need to be smoothed out and polished so we can more acceptably serve Him. But Jonah was no new-comer; he had already been a successful prophet (2 Kings 14:23-25). Even mature servants, however, need to grow and develop. There is always room for improvement, and Jonah, as you can tell from his life-story, was no exception.

Jonah is a classic example of a servant of God who put his will above the will of God—who thought, in this particular part of his life, that he knew better than God. Thus, in the first chapter we see him as presumptuous, disobeying God's command to go to Nineveh and preach against it. In chapter two, because of God's dealings with him (using the "steam-roller" approach), Jonah desperately vows to turn back to doing God's will. In chapter three, God honors his vow and recommissions him to preach in Nineveh. Jonah gives instant obedience. Chapter four, however, demonstrates that obedience is not always a guarantee of a right spirit or attitude. Jonah, the most successful evangelist-prophet of the Old Testament, is displeased with the outcome! He is angry over the conversion of an entire city! Jonah is in desperate need of correction, and our loving Lord is going to see that he gets it. He loves Jonah too much to let him get away with his unfounded anger. He corrects us that way too when we need it.

B. THE PURPOSE OF THE BOOK OF JONAH

Jonah is the author of his own story. Perhaps we can picture him returning to Gath-hepher, having learned the lessons that God intended for his erring servant, having been humbled by the truth which God used to correct him (4:1-11). Of course, the story of Jonah ends rather abruptly and does not reveal the effect of God's correcting ministry on Jonah. This has led some to believe that Jonah continued in his bitterness. *But if Jonah wrote this book, he must have responded to the correcting dialogue that he had with the Lord. After all, he is telling on himself!* Only a restored servant would have the humility to do this. He went to his home and wrote out his story so that his people might have an understanding of God's gracious heart of love to all sinners—even wicked Gentiles like the Ninevites. It is very sad, in the light of the repentance of a whole Gentile city, that one of the most difficult lessons for Jonah's own people to learn was that of repentance from sin. Is this a problem with us?

OUTLINE OF THE BOOK

The outline is based on the theme—Jonah, himself, in relation to the will of God in his service as a prophet.

1. THE PRESUMPTION OF JONAH—
Disobedience to the will of God 1

a. The PRELUDE to his disobedience to the will of God 1:1-2

The prelude to his disobedience is the commission which God laid upon him. That commission was to go 500 miles northeast to wicked Nineveh, capital of the strong and cruel Assyrian empire, located on the eastern bank of the Tigris River, and preach against it. What an awesome commission! But what a wonderful privilege to be used by God in His service!

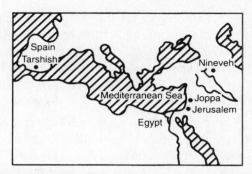

b. **The PATH of his disobedience to the will of God** 1:3

   (1) In terms of service—"Jonah rose up to flee **FROM THE
   PRESENCE OF THE LORD.**" This expression does not
   mean that Jonah thought he could go somewhere where
   God was not. Rather, he was fleeing from the presence of
   the Lord in the sense that he was throwing off the
   responsibility of his prophetic office (compare 2 Chronicles
   29:11; Psalm 51:10-11). We can never get out of God's
   presence, for He is everywhere (Psalm 139), but we can
   refuse to do His will.

   (2)   In terms of geography—"down to Joppa . . . ship to
   Tarshish . . ." Jonah was fleeing from his hometown of
   Gath-hepher to Joppa which was 50 miles down from the
   hills of Galilee on the sea shore. Joppa was the only sea
   port on the coast of Palestine in Jonah's day. He boarded a
   ship which was sailing to Tarshish. This means that he
   would rather go 2,000 miles west in disobedience, than
   500 miles northeast in obedience to the will of God. He
   paid the fare and climbed on board. Jonah was using God's
   money to further his sin and rebellion. His physical action
   of going "down" is quite illustrative of his spiritual
   condition. The path of disobedience is always down.

c. **The PROBLEMS encountered by his disobedience
   to the will of God** 1:4-17

Jonah is *pursued* by God in the storm (1:4-5); he is *rebuked* by the
captain when found in a deep sleep during the storm (1:6); he is
exposed by the casting of "lots" and found to be the culprit

responsible for these dire straits (1:7); he is *interrogated* by the sailors who became "extremely frightened" when they learned of Jonah's rebellion (1:8-12); and finally, he is *disciplined* by God in the great fish (1:13-17) after the sailors threw him overboard. "The Lord had appointed a great fish to swallow Jonah, and Jonah was in the stomach of the fish three days and three nights."

When God's servants rebel, they can expect to be pursued by Him. It is important that we have the right perspective on God's pursuit of Jonah. It was not a pursuit of retaliation, but a pursuit of love. God was not saying, "Jonah has done me wrong and I'm going to see to it that he gets hurt." Many people picture God in this way. It is a poor and unbiblical concept of God. God pursues Jonah because He loves Jonah. Rebellion and disobedience are self-destructive and God doesn't want Jonah to destroy himself. Rebellion and disobedience often adversely affect the lives of other also, although, in this case, the mariners did accept Jehovah as their Savior. We must see God as a Father who is seeking the recovery and restoration of His servant.

This story is literally true. There is absolutely no reason why we should think of it as a fictional allegory or parable. It happened just as it is told. If you took God out of the story of Jonah, then the story would be impossible, but let the omnipotent God have His proper place in this book and there is no problem. All the objections to taking Jonah as a literal, historical story have been adequately answered by conservative scholarship. Let God be God! Is God able to hurl a wind and storm upon the sea? Is He able to prepare a fish that could accommodate a man and keep the man alive for as long as seventy-two hours?" The answer is obvious.

2. **THE PRAYER OF JONAH**—Desperation to get back

The Lord has pursued His rebellious servant into the sea. Jonah was out of the will of God but he was never out of God's sight or care. God in His Fatherly role is correcting His erring child by casting him into the sea and incarcerating him in the belly of the great fish. Jonah does what any of us would do in a time like this (a time of complete helplessness). He calls out to the only One who can help him. The One he is running from is the One he now runs to—Jehovah his God.

There are a few things we should observe about his prayer. *First, the form used.* It is poetic (vv. 2-9). We must be clear that Jonah did not pray in poetic form while inside the fish. He prayed as any man would in any desperate situation. But later, when he wrote this book by the inspiration of the Holy Spirit, he put his prayer into poetic form— just like the prayers found in the book of Psalms. *Second, there are three major sections* to this written prayer.

a. The Introduction 2:1

As you can observe, the introduction is in prose and gives the location from which he prayed—"stomach of the fish."

b. The Prayer, Itself 2:2-9

This is developed in three movements:

(1) First Movement—2:2-4

Distress, 2; Confession, 3-4a; Confidence, 4b

(2) Second Movement—2:5-6

Distress, 5-6a; Confession, 6b-7a; Confidence, 7b

(3) Third Movement—2:7-9

Testimony, 8; Thanksgiving, 9a; Exclamation, 9b

c. The Conclusion 2:10

This, like the introduction, is in prose. It tells of his release from the great fish, "vomited . . . onto the dry land." Feinberg says, "In all probability the dry land upon which Jonah was cast was the coast of Palestine near Joppa. According to Jonah's faith, so was it unto him: the deliverance he had taken by faith in the fish is now realized and viewed by sight."

It should be remembered that in this chapter, Jonah becomes a type of our Lord Jesus Christ (see Matt. 12:40) in His burial and resurrection. The Lord Jesus Christ affirms that Jonah was an actual historical figure who actually experienced incarceration in, and deliverance from, the great fish. No one can improve on our Lord's evaluation.

Sometimes the only way a self-willed person can be straightened out is by the "steam-roller" approach—that is, by severe affliction and trial. May we learn early to be submissive to the will of God, not just because he may severely deal with us if we aren't, but because God's will is true wisdom, and it is the best for us, even if we do not understand it.

3. THE PREACHING OF JONAH—
Obedience to the will of God 3:1-10

Jonah has come out of the fish well-chastened. What he was unwilling to do at first, he is now instantly willing to accomplish—preach to the Ninevites. It should be noted, however, that though Jonah is willing, he has the wrong attitude. This attitude erupts in chapter four. Nevertheless, his success is phenomenal in his city-wide campaign. Present-day evangelistic results pale before the preaching of this Old Testament evangelist.

a. Jonah Re-Commissioned 3:1-2

As you can see, God doesn't give up on His servants easily. Yes, Jonah has failed, but God is not through with him! This should be an encouragement to us. Remember, when you fail in His service, pick up the pieces and go on (remember John Mark?).

b. Jonah's Willingness 3:3

Instant obedience was his response, just as there had been instant disobedience. But as we have said, his attitude was bad.

c. Jonah's Method 3:4a

The NASV says, "Then Jonah began to go through the city one day's walk." Jonah walked through the city preaching on the streets and in the squares. He went where the people were (this is what Paul did in the book Acts). He didn't rent a building or raise a tent. Do we go where the fish are?

d. Jonah's Message 3:4b

As we have it in the English Bible, his message is just eight words: "YET FORTY DAYS AND NINEVEH SHALL BE OVERTHROWN." Is this meant to be just a summary of what he preached, or is it all he preached? We do not know, but we do understand that the message was conditional—that is, God will spare them if they repent and believe (compare 3:5-10).

e. Jonah's Success 3:5-10

The whole city was converted, from the King down to the common people. It was true conversion. How do we know? Because "God saw their deeds, that they turned from their wicked way." Their belief (v. 5) and repentance were sincere. Man looks on the outward appearance, but God looks on the heart. Thus, because they repented, God repented. *Because they changed their minds about sin and God, God changed His method in dealing with them.* God is holy; He could have dealt with Nineveh in wrath and destruction. God is also love, and He can deal with them in grace and salvation. His dealings with Nineveh depended upon whether they repented or not. Because they repented of sin and turned to God, God repented (changed his mind) in *how* he would deal with them. Thus, He saved them instead of destroying them. See the two methods:

GOD	
HOLY	LOVE
WRATH	GRACE
DESTRUCTION	SALVATION

Jonah's message of judgment was a *contingency* prophecy. In other words, how God treated Nineveh was contingent upon Nineveh's response. Would they continue in sin, or would they repent? Much of Old Testament prophecy is contingency prophecy (See Joel 2:12-17; Amos 5).

4. THE DISPLEASURE OF JONAH—Embittered
by the will of God 4:1-11

The conversion of Nineveh in chapter three is one of God's great miracles in the Bible. Most evangelists today would like to have been in Jonah's place! Unfortunately, Jonah was a miserable wretch instead of a rejoicing saint. He now shows this misery by angrily voicing his complaint to God.

a. The STATEMENT of his Displeasure 4:1

The NASV says, "But it greatly displeased Jonah, and he became angry"—literally, "it was *evil* to Jonah, a great evil." (EVIL is seen to be a crushing, an affliction or injury.) The word "angry" is literally, HOT-TEMPERED. Jonah is having a temper-tantrum! A person has a temper-tantrum when his will is crossed; he loses all patience. Jonah will show his hot temper in his prayer that follows.

b. The PRAYER of his Displeasure 4:2-4

This is an "I told you so" prayer (4:2). In it he reveals the basis of his motive for not wanting to go to Nineveh—the CHARACTER OF GOD! "For I knew that Thou art a gracious and compassionate God, slow to anger and abundant in lovingkindness, AND ONE WHO RELENTS CONCERNING CALAMITY." He didn't want to preach to the Ninevites because he knew that if they repented, God would spare them, and Jonah didn't want them spared!

He now makes an angry request. It is the type of request that comes from one who is having a temper-tantrum because he has not gotten his own way: "Therefore now, O LORD, please take my life from me, for death is better to me than life." This plea for death shows two things about Jonah, and these two things are two dominant elements that are always found in those who act contrary to God's will: (1) A lack of CONFIDENCE IN GOD'S WISDOM. Does God really know that He is doing? Doesn't He know that His pardon of the Ninevites will rebound on Him? Unfortunately, Jonah thought he knew better than God. (2) A lack of SUBMISSION TO THE WILL OF GOD. The two go hand in hand. Moses and Elijah had expressed a death wish, but they spoke out of despondency in God's service. Jonah spoke out of personal hurt and injury.

How beautifully God answers Jonah: "And the LORD said, Do you have good reason to be angry?" It is a question of gentle reproof, given in the spirit of correction, not condemnation. Its purpose is to cool Jonah down, and to get him to take an unemotional look at the unreasonableness of his anger. God is dealing with him as a father would with his child. This is how He deals with us.

c. **The CORRECTION of his Displeasure** 4:5-11

Jonah goes outside the city where he makes himself a shelter of twigs and branches. There he waits, and there God teaches him a very valuable lesson through the use of the "plant" and the "east wind." That lesson is found in verses 10 and 11. God points out the wrongness of Jonah's spiritual unconcern for human welfare in contrast with his selfish concern for his own physical welfare. Jonah pitied an inanimate object, (a gourd), but God pitied Nineveh. Jonah did not labor for the plant, but God had created the people of Nineveh (and had given them their well being.) The plant came up in a night and disappeared, but the souls of the Ninevites are eternal. Jonah must have profited by this correction since he afterwards wrote the story. Have you profited by it? Do you have an impartial love for all mankind? Do you love your neighbor?

CONCLUSION

It is wonderful to know that our God loves us. His love is seen quite clearly in the story of Jonah. It is a love that seeks our best, even when that love must cause us some pain. Always keep in mind that God does not treat His children and servants as He does a lost world. This can be seen by contrasting Jonah with Nineveh:

GOD

NINEVEH	JONAH
To them, God is the moral Governor of the universe.	To him, God is a loving, correcting Father and Master.
They are ungodly sinners.	He is a beloved child and servant.
They are under the threat of eternal retribution.	He is under the experience of chastisement which is only for time.
The threat of judgment is geared to force a decision to repent.	The chastisement is geared to bring a correction and alteration in Jonah's conduct.
This is with a view to God's glory and the good of Nineveh which is salvation.	This is with a view of God's glory and the good of Jonah who needs maturing in his faith.

Let us have a healthy, Scriptural understanding of God's attitude and actions towards us. This will stimulate us to love and serve Him more.

4

The Book of Amos

Do you respect a man with courage? Do you admire a man who not only has well-founded convictions but who stands up for what he believes? Do you appreciate a man who is willing, no matter what the cost—even death—to speak that which is true, though it may not be popular with the majority? Do you love a man who not only has a keen sense of justice but who is willing, in the face of stern opposition, to stand up for the rights and needs of the powerless and poor? If your answer is yes, then Amos is your man! He was all these things as a servant of the Lord—and more. He was a dynamic personality who exploded onto the public scene in a day when society, religion and government were bankrupt. What a terrific indictment he delivered! How it convicted all who heard it! We wish that God would raise up others like him to speak out against our corrupt society and nation, and to call men and women back to Himself. Let's study this man and his book to see what motivated him to be the man for God that he was. Will his life and prophecies challenge us to turn from our wicked ways and return to heart-felt devotion to Jesus Christ? May it be so for His glory!

I. THE MAN, AMOS

A. HIS NAME

The name *Amos* means "burden-bearer." What an appropriate name, for he was a bearer of the burden of judgment to several nations, as well as to Judah and Israel. He is the only man in the Old Testament with this name. Do not confuse him with Amoz who was the father of the prophet Isaiah. Though the great majority of the book has to do with the judgment of God, there is a wonderful closing prophecy concerning the future restoration of Israel. Even in the midst of judgment there is grace (9:11-15).

B. HIS HOMETOWN

Not all the prophets were from a big city. Some were born and brought up in Jerusalem, in the shadow of the temple and palace (Isaiah), but others in relative obscurity, like Amos. Tekoa was the town from which this courageous prophet arose. It was in the tribal area of Judah (see map), in the Southern Kingdom. It was near Jerusalem, just 12 miles south of this capital of the Southern Kingdom (Amos would not preach there). From

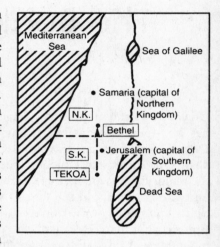

this tiny village, bounded by limestone hills, you could look east eighteen miles and see clearly the Dead Sea 4,000 feet below. Tekoa was a wild, desolate, deserted spot. The lonely hills provided the physical atmosphere for some of the training of this prophet. His personality was somewhat like the surroundings in which he grew up—rugged and tough. This was just the kind of man that God needed to preach His word of judgment at Bethel.

C. HIS OCCUPATION

Some people need to hold two jobs to support themselves. A resident of Tekoa like Amos had a hard time making ends meet. He was a "herdman, and a gatherer of sycomore fruit" (Amos 7:14b). The "sycomore" bore a low-grade fig-like fruit. This fruit had to be pierced before it could be gathered from the trees in order to get rid of the insects that infest it. This was a seasonal occupation. At various times of the year Amos would journey to those areas of Palestine where the trees were farmed (coastal plain or the Jordan valley). Cultivating sycomore fruit was among the lowest of occupations in Palestine, so we are reminded of Amos' poor economic condition. But though he was poor in this world, "he was rich in faith." Amos' migrant work took him into the Northern Kingdom. Little did he realize that one day he would go to the Northern Kingdom, not to pick fruit, but to preach God's message at Bethel.

D. HIS MINISTRY

We shall observe several things concerning his ministry. Amos is not mentioned in the books of 2 Kings or 2 Chronicles, but his own prophecy provides much information which accords with the history of the Kings.

1. **The Time of His Ministry** (Compare 1:1 with 7:10-17; 2 Kings 14:23)

    Generally, Amos prophesied during the kingships of Jeroboam II, king of Israel (Northern Kingdom), and Uzziah, king of Judah (Southern Kingdom). Please refer to your chart of the kings where the dates of these two kings are given. You will see that Amos was an eighth century BC prophet like Jonah, Hosea, Isaiah, and Micah. Jeroboam II reigned for over forty years and was a wicked king: "AND HE DID THAT WHICH WAS EVIL IN THE SIGHT OF THE LORD: HE DEPARTED NOT FROM ALL THE SINS OF JEROBOAM (the first) THE SON OF NEBAT, WHO MADE ISRAEL TO SIN" (2 Kings 14:24). Even to such a wicked, idolatrous king, God showed His grace, for Jonah prophesied military prosperity for him (2 Kings 14:25). The goodness of God was meant to lead him to reprentance, but it had no effect on him (compare Romans 2:4). Do not be deceived into thinking that God's goodness to us is necessarily to be interpreted as His approval of our conduct. The political, religious, social and material corruption of the reign of Jeroboam II is well reflected in such passages as Amos 4:1-5; 5:11, 12; 5:21-27; 6:1-6; 7:7-9; 8:1-6.

    Specifically, Amos prophesied *"TWO YEARS BEFORE THE EARTH QUAKE"* (1:1). Arnold Schultz says, "The statement, 'two years before the earthquake,' indicates more precisely the time of his ministry because it refers to an earthquake which, it appears, was accompanied by a total eclipse (5:8; Zechariah 14:5, 6). Such a phenomenom took place in 763 BC. It would appear, then, that approximately 760 BC, or the last half of Jeroboam's reign, when the evil forces set in motion by the king were bearing their rotten fruit, is the time of Amos' great career" (Biblical Expositor, Vol. 2, page 302). Could it be that God is calling you to preach His word? Don't be anxious. The time will come, God's time when, just as Amos, you will step out to declare the whole counsel of God. In the meantime, "wait on the Lord: be of good courage, and he shall strengthen thine heart: wait, I say, on the Lord" (Psalm 27:14).

2.   **The Call to His Ministry** (Amos 7:10-17; 3:8)

"Then answered Amos, and said to Amaziah, I was no prophet, neither was I a prophet's son; but I was a herdsman, and a gatherer of sycamore fruit: *AND THE LORD TOOK ME AS I FOLLOWED THE FLOCK, AND THE LORD SAID UNTO ME, GO, PROPHESY UNTO MY PEOPLE ISRAEL."* Then again, in 3:8, "The Lion hath roared, who will not fear? THE LORD GOD HATH SPOKEN, WHO CAN BUT PROPHESY?" Amos had no training as a prophet. He was not a professional prophet ("I was no prophet"), nor was he a member of the schools of the prophets ("neither was I a prophet's son"). That made no difference because he was CALLED OF THE LORD! It is God's calling that makes the prophet! Heritage and education are fine, but they do not account for, or take the place of, the call of God.

It is interesting to note that it was while Amos was involved in his occupation of shepherding that God's call came. Many of God's saints in our day have had a similar experience. Engaged in secular work, they never dreamed that one day God would call them into whole-time service for Him.

Remember those fishermen in the gospels to whom the Lord said, "FOLLOW ME, AND I WILL MAKE YOU FISHERS OF MEN. *AND THEY STRAIGHTWAY LEFT THEIR NETS, AND FOLLOWED HIM"* (Matt. 4:19, 20). Will you be ready if God calls you?

3. The Place of His Ministry—Bethel

This Southern Kingdom prophet was commissioned by God to preach in the Northern Kingdom city of Bethel. Bethel had an illustrious background. Abraham had encamped there (Genesis 12:8). Later, Jacob had there dreamed his famous dream (Genesis 28:10-22) which motivated him to give the name "Bethel" (house of God) to the place, which had formerly been called Luz (Genesis 28:19). However, when the United Kingdom was divided in 931 BC (see 1 Kings 12-14), Bethel became one of the two major religious sites of the Northern Kingdom (2 Kings 12:25-31). There the idolatrous worship of the golden calf was established and continued to the end of the Northern Kingdom. Thus, Bethel (the house of God) became a house of iniquity. It was to this place (Amos 7:10-13) that Amos brought his awesome indictment. There are many such "sin cities" in our nation and throughout the world which began with a grand religious heritage but have become dens of iniquity. Praise God for the power of the gospel which is reaching these places and rescuing men and women from destruction. Will you be used in this kind of mission?

We have surveyed the TIME, CALL, AND PLACE of Amos' ministry. If God CALLS you, He will make the TIME and PLACE clear. "Wait on the Lord." But always remember, we do not have to be in whole-time service to serve Him acceptably and successfully. "Whatsoever thy hand findeth to do, do it with all thy might."

II. THE BOOK OF AMOS

THE THEME OF THE BOOK

It only takes one reading of the book of Amos to discover that its theme is the *JUDGMENT OF GOD.* God is a *JUST* God, and when His holy laws are violated He acts impartially in judgment upon those who will not repent and receive His mercy. Several nations surrounding Palestine, plus Judah (Southern Kingdom) and Israel (Northern Kingdom) are threatened with His judgment. But it is sinful Israel that is primarily in view in the book. The judgment messages delivered to the Northern Kingdom at Bethel are contingency prophecies—that is, if Israel will repent, then the judgment of God will be stayed! God had already been chastising the Northern Kingdom (4:6-11), but now He threatens its destruction and the exile of its people (3:11-15; 4:2, 3; 4:12-13; 5:1-3, 11, 16-27; 6:7-14; 7:7-9; 8:1-3; 9:1-10). Of course, we know that Israel did not repent; these prophecies were fulfilled by God, using the cruel Assyrian nation as the instrument of His judgment (2 Kings 15-17). "Be not deceived; God is not mocked; for whatsoever a man (or a nation) soweth, that shall he also reap" (Galatians 6:7). The nation that forgets God and goes its own way will reap what it has sowed.

It is interesting to observe several parallels between Amos and the New Testament book of Romans regarding the theme of judgment. The Jews of Paul's day, though not given to overt idolatry—bowing down to images, etc.—were very self-righteous and felt that God would not judge them as He would the Gentile nations. Paul expounds several principles of judgment in Romans 2–3 to clear up this faulty thinking. All of these principles can be found in Amos. Let us note them:

Judgment is *WITHOUT RESPECT OF PERSON* (Amos 1-2 c.f. Romans 2:11)

Judgment is *ACCORDING TO ONE'S LIGHT* (Amos 3:1-2 c.f. Romans 2:12)

Judgment is *FOREWARNED* (Amos 4:2, 12 c.f. Romans 2:5)

Judgment is *CONDITIONAL* (Amos 5:4, 6, 8, 14 c.f. Romans 2:7)

Judgment is *CERTAIN* (Amos 6 c.f. Romans 2:3)

Judgment is *INESCAPABLE* (Amos 9:1-10 c.f. Romans 2:3, 16)

God has only one standard of judgment. He will judge all people by that one standard in accordance with the light they have. The Jews were the most enlightened nation in the world. Much then, would be required from them.

OUTLINE

The outline of Amos is based on the theme, THE JUDGMENT OF GOD. It is easily traced:

1. EIGHT PROPHETIC BURDENS OF JUDGMENT 1-2

2. THREE SERMONS OF JUDGMENT 3-6

3. FIVE VISIONS OF JUDGMENT 7-9

4. RESTORATION 9:11-15

just like Joel and Obadiah.

1. EIGHT PROPHETIC BURDENS OF JUDGMENT 1-2

Remember that Amos is preaching these messages at Bethel, the main religious center of the Northern Kingdom. This courageous prophet not only lashes out at six neighboring nations of Palestine (Syria, Philistia, Phoenicia, Edom, Ammon, and Moab), but he turns the spotlight of condemnation also upon Judah and Israel (2:4-16). Observe their location on the map.

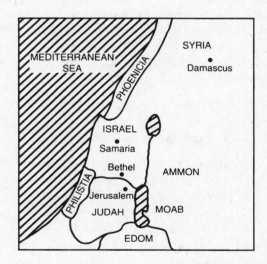

The people of Bethel must have applauded Amos as he condemned the surrounding nations for their sins, and spoke of the judgment coming upon them (1:3-2:3); they must have said a loud "AMEN" to Amos' denunciation of the rival Southern Kingdom of Judah! But when he righteously pointed the finger of judgment at the Northern Kingdom of which they were citizens, we know from the rest of the book that they hated him for this (5:10; 7:10-17). Amos was impartial.

He said what he had to say—the truth—and was not intimidated by what their response might be. He did not seek for popularity; he would not water down his message. He was truly God's prophet— "let the chips fall where they may". Is that the kind of witness we are for Christ? Or are we afraid of what others may say, or do, to us?

The nations were guilty of great cruelty and injustice, but the guilt of Judah and Israel was greater, for they had been blessed with the truth of God and should have been living in the light of it.

2. THREE SERMONS OF JUDGMENT 3-6

From general messages of judgment, Amos now specifically speaks to the Northern Kingdom in a series of three sermons. These sermons have many similarities: (1) each has the same beginning ("hear this word"), (2) each contains severe rebukes, (3) each speaks of the judgment God will bring if they don't repent, (4) each has some element which should have spoken to Israel to turn back to God, and (5) each has some pathetic expression of the spiritual condition of the Northern Kingdom. See if you can discover these.

a. FIRST JUDGMENT SERMON 3

(1) The People to Be Judged 3:1

It is the chosen people—the people God had redeemed and delivered from Egypt. How thankful they should have been, and how they should have shown this thanks by godly living.

(2) The Principles of Judgment 3:2

"You only have I *known* of all the families of the earth: THEREFORE I WILL PUNISH YOU FOR ALL YOUR INIQUITIES." The principle is clear: *God judges people and nations in accordance with the light they have.* Israel, being God's chosen, had more light than any other nation. Privilege brings responsibility. They had great light, so they should have lived accordingly. Failure to do this brings greater judgment. From those to whom much is given, much will be required.

(3) **The Preacher of Judgment**—Amos 3:3-8

As you can discern from 7:10-17, Amos' right or authority to preach in the Northern Kingdom was challenged by Amaziah, the priest of Bethel. Amaziah said, "Who do you think you are, Amos, to come up to our kingdom and preach against the king and the people. Go back where you came from, for you have no right to be here!" But Amos, using several *CAUSE AND EFFECT ILLUSTRATIONS* (3:3-8a) justifies his calling to preach: *"THE LORD GOD HATH SPOKEN, WHO CAN BUT PROPHESY?"* (3:8b).

(4) **The Justification for Judgment** 3:9-10

Sin is the absolute justification for the coming judgment. This is summed up in the sentence, *"For they know not to do right,* saith the Lord," (v. 10). What an awful condition! How terribly far they had fallen!

(5) **The Plan for Judgment** 3:11-15

What punitive measures will God bring upon Israel? "Therefore thus saith the Lord God; *an adversary* there shall be even round about the land; and he shall bring down thy strength (fortress) from thee, and thy palaces shall be spoiled" (v. 11). This *adversary* was the Assyrian nation (see 2 Kings 15-17) who eventually destroyed the Northern Kingdom in 722 BC. God sometimes uses nations as a chastising instrument (see Daniel 2, 7). Samaria, the political capital, and Bethel, the religious capital, will meet their end.

Is our nation any better than Israel of old? What light we have from God! But does God say of us: "They know not to do right?"

b. **SECOND JUDGMENT SERMON** 4

The awful depravity of Israel is vividly described in this sermon. It is a picture of how low a nation can go morally, religiously and spiritually.

(1) MORALLY—The Cruel Women of Israel 4:1-3

These women are the high society women of the Northern Kingdom. They are the wives of the leaders and officials. They have power because their husbands have power. They have a continual lust for more. They are never satisfied. Amos calls them "cows of Bashan." They are morally bankrupt as is evidenced by their oppressing and crushing of the poor and needy in order to maintain their expensive and luxurious life-style. Amos warns them they will be led away like animals when the judgment comes! Every society has women like this. They will not escape God's judgment.

(2) RELIGIOUSLY—The Corrupt Worship of Israel 4:4-6

God had not ordained the religion of the Northern Kingdom. Its religious sites (Bethel, Dan, Gilgal) were a continual scandal to the heavens, as idolatry and immorality were constantly practiced. Amos speaks ironically in verse four: "Go on, then, and get on with your sinning; go to Gilgal, and pile up your sins" (Phillips, Four Prophets, MacMillan, p. 11). The religious pilgrimages to these sites were not "holy" but sinful, but, as Phillips puts it, "this is what you love to do" (v. 5).

(3) SPIRITUALLY—The Calloused Will of Israel 4:7-13

Because of their continued sin, God had chastised them with famine (v. 6), drought (vv. 7-8), pestilence (vv. 9-10a), and warfare (vv. 10b-11). In a sense, these were all acts of love from a concerned Father with the design to make them hurt so they would awaken to their awful spiritual condition. How did they respond? A repeated sentence gives the answer: "YET HAVE YE NOT RETURNED UNTO ME, SAITH THE LORD" (vv. 6, 8, 9, 10, 11). *Their will is calloused!* What an awful condition for any child of God. To get to the place where the will does not respond to the Lord! Let us determine that we shall stay sensitive to His voice! He greatly loves us and seeks only our good.

Amos closes this message of judgment by challenging Israel: "PREPARE TO MEET THY GOD, O ISRAEL." He then describes the God they must prepare to meet (verse 13): He is the mighty, powerful Creator. He is not like humans who many times can threaten but have no power to carry through. He can accomplish His Word!

c. THIRD JUDGMENT SERMON 5-6

This judgment message is made up of Lamentation, Exhortation and Warning.

(1) THE GRIEVOUS LAMENTATION 5:1-3

This song is a funeral dirge: "The virgin of Israel is fallen; she shall no more rise: she is forsaken upon her land; there is none to raise her up" (v. 2). Amos sees no hope!

Though her destruction has not come, it is as good as done! But though the outlook is pessimistic, Amos has not finished preaching the grace of God; he continues with an exhortation (vv. 4-15).

(2) THE GRACIOUS EXHORTATION 5:4-17

Is there any hope for such a wicked nation? Yes, the offer of grace is extended. This is seen in the word "SEEK" (vv. 4, 5, 6, 8, 14). Seek the Lord . . . seek good and not evil, that ye may live." (5:6, 14) The judgment is coming (at the hands of the Assyrians), but it can be averted if they will repent. They have gone far in idolatry and social injustice, but God's grace goes further (see Romans 5:20, 21). But what if they don't repent? Then they can only expect the worst (vv. 16-17a) "for I will pass through thee, saith the Lord." God passed through Egypt (Exodus 12) and the firstborn perished. This time judgment was to fall on Israel.

(3) THE GRIM WARNING—"Woe . . . Woe . . ." 5:18-6:14

(a) THE FIRST WOE 5:18-27

This woe is "the day of the Lord" (vv. 18, 20). When Israel thinks of "the day of the Lord," they think only of God's intervention in their behalf to deliver them from their enemy. But He warns them that this time they will be delivered to the enemy. And if they think that refuge can be found in their religion, they are mistaken, for God hates it (vv. 21-27). Therefore, they shall "go into captivity beyond Damascus." How deceived they are to think that God approves of a religion which is void of morality! God says, "LET JUDGMENT RUN AS WATERS, AND RIGHTEOUSNESS AS A MIGHTY STREAM" (v. 24). Are we Christians? Then let us be holy and righteous in all our dealings.

(b) THE SECOND WOE 6

This woe is directed toward their false confidence. When Amos preached, the Northern Kingdom was strong militarily and very wealthy. King Jeroboam II was on the throne. The ruling class was at ease, trusting in its success and in its well-fortified stronghold of Samaria (this was even the case in Judah-Zion, v. 1). This success caused them to "put far away the evil day," (v. 3)—to think that nothing bad could happen to them. It is so easy, isn't it, when things are going well, to think that God's stamp of approval is upon us. But while the rich ruling class lived in the lap of luxury, pampering themselves with every sensual delight, the poor were oppressed. Amos tells the rich that, since they have been first in everything in life, God would see to it that they are *first in judgment* (6:7).

3. FIVE VISIONS OF JUDGMENT 7-9

The last three chapters, with the exception of the Epilogue, continue the theme of judgment. This time the form of the revelation is *vision*. Amos not only hears the communication of God's word, but he *sees it*. A historical interlude comes between the third and fourth vision, having to do with the dialogue between Amos and Amaziah (7:10-17). Each of these visions conveys a certain aspect of judgment in a progressive form.

THE VISIONS 7:9-10

a. JUDGMENT AVERTED—Vision of Devouring Locusts and Consuming Fire 7:1-6

As Amos sees these awesome judgments, his heart melts within him, causing him to intercede in Israel's behalf that they be removed. God answers his prayers affirmatively. This is the case of "an effectual, fervent prayer of a righteous man availing much" (James 5:16).

b. JUDGMENT DETERMINED—Vision of the
Plumbline 7:7-9

The first two visions were in the realm of nature. This one has to do with the national life of Israel. Israel is measured politically and religiously and is found crooked. Amos does not intercede, for the Lord is determined that He will not again pass by them any more" (v. 8). The house (dynasty) of Jeroboam II will fall: "I will rise up against the house of Jeroboam with the sword." (v. 9)

c. HISTORICAL INTERLUDE 7:10-17

This interlude is probably placed here because it follows the third vision chronologically. Amaziah, the priest of Bethel, tells Amos to leave and go to the south to prophecy. Amos holds his ground and prophesies judgment against Amaziah and his family. Amaziah is illustrative of all false religionists who sell themselves to the powers-that-be in order to maintain the lifestyle they desire. Of course, all true prophets of God are seen as a threat to them.

d. JUDGMENT INEVITABLE—Vision of the Basket
of Summer Fruit 8:1-14

Israel is like a basket of over-ripe summer fruit. Just as the fruit is good for nothing and will be thrown out on the garbage heap, so Israel is good for nothing and the inevitable will come: "The end is come upon my people of Israel; I will not again pass by them any more" (8:2).

e. JUDGMENT IS INESCAPABLE—Vision of the
Lord on the Altar at Bethel 9:1-10

The Lord is pictured as ready to smite Israel, and when He does this, no one will escape. This last vision is breathtaking as the Lord personally enters the sinful scene. "It is a fearful thing to fall into the hands of the living God!" (Hebrews 10:31) But in this last vision, there is a ray of hope: "BEHOLD, THE EYES OF THE LORD GOD ARE UPON THE SINFUL KINGDOM, AND I WILL DESTROY IT FROM OFF THE FACE OF THE EARTH; *SAVING THAT I WILL NOT UTTERLY DESTROY THE HOUSE OF JACOB, SAITH THE LORD.*" It is this promise that is pictured in the Epilogue (9:11-15).

4. RESTORATION 9:11-15

Like Obadiah and Joel, Amos ends his prophecy on a positive note concerning the future restoration of Israel.

a. The Restoration of the Davidic Dynasty 9:11a

"I will raise up the tabernacle (house, dynasty) of David that is fallen" (compare Acts 15:16-17). This refers to the restoration of the Davidic house when Jesus will sit on the throne of David (see Luke 1:31-33). The passage in Acts does not mean that the tabernacle of David is the Church!

b. The Restoration of Unity in the Nation 9:11b-12

"And close up the breaches thereof; and I will raise up his ruins, and I will build it as in the days of old." The Kingdom was divided in 931 BC. The breach was made then, but in the future day the nation will be unified again under the Messiah (see Hosea 1:9-10; Ezekiel 37:15ff).

c. The Restoration of Agriculture 9:13

"Behold, the days come, saith the LORD, that the plowman shall overtake the reaper, and the treader of grapes him that soweth seed; and the mountains shall drop sweet wine, and all the hills shall melt." So fertile will the soil be that the plowman, preparing the soil for the next harvest will overtake the reaper. "In other words, seedtime and harvest will follow in rapid succession, without interruption of this process through drought or any other plague. The hills, normally barren, will also make their contribution to the prosperity of the people, for they shall yield their harvest of grapes" (O. Bussey).

d. The Restoration of the People 9:14a

"And I will bring again the captivity of my people Israel, and they shall build the waste cities, and inhabit them." This refers to the restoration of captives from all over the world where Israel has been scattered (see Ezekiel 36:24).

e. The Restoration of Liberty 9:14b

"And they shall plant vineyards, and *drink the wine thereof;* they shall also make gardens, and eat 'fruit of them.' In that day they will be in control of their own produce. They won't be growing it to give to some other nation as tribute, but will enjoy it themselves."

f. The Restoration Is Permanent 9:15

"And I will plant them upon their land, and they shall no more be pulled up out of their land which I have given them, saith the LORD thy God."

What a day that will be! Israel back in the land permanently! When that happens, there will be peace. No more will God's ancient people live in fear.

God delights to bless His people! Do you need restoration from sin? Why not repent now and start anew? God longs to fill your life with blessing. Let Him do it. Let Him do it now!

5

The Book of Hosea

How would you like it if the Lord spoke to you one day and said, "I am going to take your beloved wife from you in death?" That's what happened to Ezekiel (24:16). How would you respond if the Lord said to you, "Young man, I am not going to let you get married. You must remain single in my service?" That is what the Lord commanded Jeremiah (16:1-4). How would you feel if you knew you were going to be fed to some fierce, hungry lions? That's what happened to the prophet Daniel (Daniel 6). How would you like it if you went to God's people to preach His message and they hated you for it and threatened your life? That happened to several of God's servants in Old Testament days (Elijah, Amos, Ezekiel, Jeremiah).

Yes, the prophets were sometimes called upon to bear great grief and suffering in the course of their ministries, and Hosea is no exception. Few prophets suffered as did this man of God. One day he stood at the altar with his beloved Gomer, the daughter of Diblaim, and they said their marriage vows to one another. He had no reason to doubt her when she promised to be loving and faithful and obedient. Their first child, Jezreel, came along, and how happy Hosea must have been. But then Gomer began to act differently toward him, and Hosea's suspicions were aroused. Finally he learned the truth about her! She had been unfaithful to the marriage vows and was running around with other lovers. How his heart was broken! How his spirit was outraged! But wonder of wonders, he never gave up loving her.

The experiences of Ezekiel and Jeremiah referred to above were designed by God to be *signs* to His people (read the passages), and the tragedy of Hosea was to be used by God as an analogy of the love relationship of God with His erring people. Little do we know what God has in store for us by way of grief and suffering, but the fact that He is *with us* and *will never leave us nor forsake us* is comforting indeed; and the fact that what we suffer in this life can be used by God to bring hope and consolation to others is very strengthening (cp. 2 Corinthians 1:1-11). Like Jeremiah, Hosea was a very sensitive man with a great heart of love. May we seek to cultivate that same unquenchable devotion to others and to our Lord.

1. THE MAN, HOSEA

A. HIS NAME

The name *HOSEA* means *Salvation*. God has been offering salvation to Israel—salvation from the domination and destruction which Hosea, and Amos before him, had proclaimed. All Israel had to do was to turn to the Lord in sincerity and repentance, and salvation would be theirs. Yes, Israel needed what Hosea's name signified—SALVATION, spiritually and otherwise. Is salvation what you need? You can have it in Jesus Christ; you can be saved from the "wrath to come" (Romans 5:9).

B. HIS PERSONAL HISTORY

1. *Location*—We know very little about where he lived. He prophesied primarily against the Northern Kingdom, and in Hosea 7:5 he speaks of "our king" which in the context is Jeroboam II, king of the Nothern Kingdom. We take it that he lived in the Northern Kingdom—possibly at Bethel or Samaria. But wherever he lived, this sensitive man, as his books reveals, found it a great burden to daily observe the apostasy of his nation. Does the holiness of God mean so much to us that, like Hosea, sin bothers us whenever we see it? It is so easy to get used to sin! Let us remember that we are called to holiness (1 Peter 1:15, 16).

2. *Family*—Hosea's father is mentioned in 1:1. His name was Beeri and this is the only thing we know about him. Chapters 1–3, of course, tell us of Hosea's tragic marriage to Gomer and the children she bore. There is no doubt that the first child, Jezreel, was the offspring of both Hosea and Gomer, but it would appear that the other two were the fruit of her unfaithfulness. God designed that these three children should be signs of the nation:

a. A Son, JEZREEL (1:4, 5)

The name, Jezreel, means "God scatters, God sows." It is symbolic of the coming judgment on the house (dynasty) of Jehu of which Jeroboam II was a king (see 2 Kings 15:8-11). It is also symbolic of the destruction of the Northern Kingdom, which took place in 722 BC at the hands of the Assyrians (2 Kings 17).

b. A Daughter, LO-RUHAMAH (1:6-7)

Her name means *unpitied*. The application is that when the judgment spoken of in 1:4-5 comes, no mercy will be shown to the Northern Kingdom. However, the Lord points out that Judah, the Southern Kingdom, will be spared by miraculous means (see Isaiah 18-20).

c. A Son, LO-AMMI (1:8-11)

After LO-RUHAMAH was weaned (weaning took two to three years), a son was born and named LO-AMMI. This means NOT MY PEOPLE and is symbolic of the fact that God has rejected Israel and set them aside. However, this rejection is temporary, for Hosea prophesies that in a coming day there will be a regathering, restoration and reunification of Israel and Judah, with the Messiah reigning over them (1:10-11). To summarize: Israel is heading for judgment (JEZREEL), and when it comes there will be no mercy (LO-RUHAMAH), even to the extent that they are temporarily set aside in the plans and purposes of God (LO-AMMI). Then, in a coming day this will all be reversed: from judgment to blessing; from unpitied to pitied; from "not my people" to "my people." Great will be the day of Jezreel!

HIS MINISTRY

1. THE TIME OF IT

a. Generally (1:1; see your chart of the Kings & Prophets)

The first verse of the first chapter places Hosea as an eighth century prophet along with Amos, Isaiah, and Micah.

"The word of the LORD that came unto Hosea, the son of Beeri, in the days of UZZIAH, JOTHAM, AHAZ, and HEZEKIAH, kings of Judah, and in the days of JEROBOAM (II) the son of Joash, king of Israel."

The background for these kings is found in 2 Kings 14-20.

b. Specifically

His ministry had its beginning toward the end of Jeroboam II's kingship (793-753) and continued right on through the destruction of the Northern Kingdom (722 BC) into the reign of King Hezekiah of Judah. Israel, the Northern Kingdom, is in a terrible state. *Politically*, it is snow-balling to the brink of disaster. *Religiously*, Israel is in no better shape: Calf worship and Baal worship (2:7-13; 10:5) are being practiced. *Morally*, evil of the worst kind is going on (4:11-14; cp. 9:9 with Judges 19:22 = sin of Gibeah). What heartbreak must have been Hosea's as he saw the inevitable end of his nation!

2. SECOND, THE TERMINOLOGY OF IT (KJV)

Several terms used by Hosea will bear some defining; this will greatly assist in understanding the prophecy.

a. WHOREDOMS (NASV, HARLOTRY) 1:2; 2:2, 4; 4:14

Hosea used this literally of adultery and prostitution, and metphorically of *idol worship* (which is unfaithfulness to God).

b. LOVERS—2:5, 7-13; 8:9-10

This word is used of Gomer's adulterous lovers, of Israel's idols, and of foreign alliances made with heathen nations.

c. BACKSLIDING 4:16

The idea is conveyed by the NASV: "*stubborn.*"

d. EPHRAIM—11:1, 3

Ephraim was a son of Joseph, and one of the tribal areas was named after him. After the kingdom divided, the Northern Kingdom was sometimes called by his name.

e. BETH-HAVEN—10:5

Beth-Haven means "house of iniquity" and it is a sarcastic name for Bethel (house of God). Bethel became a house of iniquity.

f. EGYPT—11:1; 9:3, 6

This refers to the literal country of Egypt in 11:1, and Hosea used it symbolically of *bondage* in 9:3, 6

g. SHALMAN—10:14

Possibly this is a short form of Shalmanezer, an Assyrian king who ruled from 727–722 BC (see 2 Kings 17:1-6).

h. JAREB—5:13; 10:6

Possibly this refers to Tiglath-Pileser III (the Pul of 2 Kings 15:19). He ruled over Assyria from 745-727 BC and like most Assyrian rulers, he was ruthless and cruel. Some, however, think this name refers to Sargon II (722-705 BC).

3. THIRD, THE RESPONSE TO IT

Many tears must have flowed from Hosea's eyes as he spoke with heart-rending conviction to his nation. But the Northern Kingdom was not impressed by the sermons of this sensitive prophet. *"The Prophet is a fool, is he, And the man inspired is a man insane"* (Phillips, Four Prophets, page 43). They looked upon him as a fool and mad, yet he preached on, for he loved those who hated him!

I. THE BOOK OF HOSEA

A. THE THEME OF THE BOOK

It is love—the *UNFAILING LOVE OF GOD TO ISRAEL*. The Song of Solomon (8:7) tells us that "MANY WATERS CANNOT QUENCH LOVE, NEITHER CAN THE FLOODS DROWN IT: IF A MAN WOULD GIVE ALL THE SUBSTANCE OF HIS HOUSE FOR LOVE, IT WOULD UTTERLY BE CONTEMNED (rejected)." God's love is real, genuine love! It is

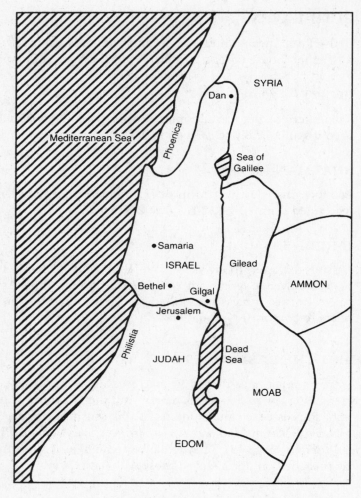

1. Samaria was the political capital of the Northern Kingdom.

2. Bethel and Dan were the chief religious sites of the Northern Kingdom.

3. Gilgal had an idolatrous shrine (12:11) in the Northern Kingdom.

a love that can NEVER BE DESTROYED. It is a love that can NEVER BE BOUGHT! This is the kind of love He has for us. Do you crave love—love that is real, a "love that will never let you go"? This is what God offers you. No matter how far we may stray, He, in His love, will pursue us to bring us back to Himself. God is unfailing in His love; that is the primary lesson of this book. This lesson is not only projected in the spoken sermons of Hosea (4-14), but is dramatized in the personal experience of his marriage and family life (1-3). Many times God used the prophets as object lessons to teach Israel some needed truth. Hosea's terrible domestic problems (caused by an unfaithful wife) brought tremendous sadness and grief to his heart, but also served to demonstrate the unquenchable devotion of love. Hosea was unfailing in his love for Gomer in spite of her adulteries. He hated, and was saddened by her sins, but he loved her from the depths of her degradation (3:1-3). In this actual, real life experience, he enacts a living drama of God's unfailing love for evil, adulterous, unfaithful Israel. This theme is developed in two sections, 1-3 and 4-14.

B. THE PROBLEM OF THE BOOK

Did God really command Hosea to marry a harlot (1:2)? Was she a harlot before he married her, or did she become one after they had been married a while? Of course, this story is to be understood literally, but among those who hold the literal view there is a difference of opinion. Some literalists hold that she was a harlot at the time Hosea married her. Notwithstanding the *moral* problem, they actually believe that the holy God commanded Hosea to do something which would be contradictory to God's holiness. Other literalists teach that when they were married, Gomer was a chaste woman and that she later became adulterous. This is the most suitable explanation of the literal view. Note the reasoning behind it:

1.   This view is proven in chapter three. There Hosea is seen as taking Gomer back to himself *after having rejected her* in chapters 1–2 for adultery. THIS REJECTION WOULD NOT SEEM JUSTIFIABLE IF HOSEA HAD MARRIED A COMMON HARLOT WITH FULL KNOWLEDGE OF HER NATURE AND PRACTICE.

2. This view fits perfectly with the analogy which the Holy Spirit gives between Jehovah and Israel: "GO take unto thee a wife of whoredoms and children of whoredoms: FOR THE LAND HATH COMMITTED GREAT WHOREDOMS, DEPARTING FROM THE LORD." (1:2). The word "land" refers to the nation. If the nation has departed from the Lord, it means that the nation was once in fellowship with the Lord. Suffice it to say that Israel was a CHASTE BRIDE when Jehovah married her at Mr. Sinai (Exodus 19). Jeremiah 2:1-3 speaks of this chastity which Israel later lost by idolatry and foreign alliances.

OUTLINE OF THE BOOK OF HOSEA

The outline of Hosea is simple in its major divisions. A clear break is seen between chapters 3 and 4. In the first three chapters Hosea and his family are prominent as part of the historical narrative symbolizing the spiritual condition of the nation. From chapter four through the end of the book Hosea's family problems disappear from sight and God's dealings with the nation are in view. However, if you learn well the traumatic experiences of Hosea in the first section (1-3), you are better able to appreciate the tremendous love of God for his habitually sinning people. You will remember that the theme of Hosea is the UNFAILING LOVE OF GOD FOR ISRAEL as dramatized in personal experience, and as expounded in sermonic form. The outline is based on this theme.

I. **THE UNFAILING LOVE OF GOD TO ISRAEL DRAMATIZED IN THE LIFE OF HOSEA AND HIS FAMILY** 1-3

A. **THE MARRIAGE AND FAMILY OF HOSEA ARE SYMBOLIC OF GOD'S RELATIONSHIP TO THE NATION OF ISRAEL** 1:1-2:1

God commanded Hosea to marry Gomer who was at the time of their wedding a chaste woman. She later became a harlot. Gomer bore three children (the second and third probably by other men) whose names were all prophetically symbolic of God's dealings with Israel— the Northern Kingdom. Remember that the symbolism was JUDGMENT . . . NO MERCY . . . AND NOT MY PEOPLE. Though the situation is very dark, the symbolism does end on a note of hope of restoration and unification for the nation (1:10-2:1). This restoration, of course, is based on the unconditional promises of God to restore His people. God is not finished with Israel!

B. THE SEPARATION OF HOSEA FROM GOMER IS SYMBOLIC OF GOD'S CHASTISEMENT OF ISRAEL FOR HER UNFAITHFULNESS 2:2-23

The *announcement* of separation is sounded: "Plead (contend) with your mother, plead: *FOR SHE IS NOT MY WIFE, NEITHER AM I HER HUSBAND . . .*" (2:2a). *This announcement is accompanied by exhortation and warning* in view of the separation: first, concerning Gomer (2:2b-3 and then her children (2:4). The *reason* for the separation is given quite clearly in 2:5: "FOR THEIR MOTHER HATH PLAYED THE HARLOT, . . ."

One cannot miss the message that Israel is to learn through this symbolism (2:6-13). God's chastening hand will be upon Israel to the extent that He will set her aside for her unfaithfulness. The chapter does end on the side of hope, for Hosea speaks of a coming day in which the Lord will seek out His erring people (2:14). When He does this, great blessing will come to Israel, and Israel will be faithful to God as she was intended to be (2:15-23).

C. THE RESTORATION OF GOMER TO HOSEA IS SYMBOLIC OF ISRAEL'S RESTORATION OF JEHOVAH IN A COMING DAY 3

The Lord who commanded Hosea to take Gomer as his wife now commands him to seek her out and take her back (3:1). BUT WHERE IS SHE? The answer is implied in 3:2: "So I *bought* her for myself for fifteen shekels of silver and a homer and a half of barley" (NASV, 3:2). If he bought her, it means that she has been a slave. She is up for sale and the price asked is very small—only half of what a slave would normally cost. What tremendous and unfailing love! After all she has done to him, he takes her back! There will be a waiting period before full marital privileges will be restored (3:3). God in His love will one day seek out unfaithful Israel (3:1b) to restore her to favor. The redemption price has already been paid in the blood of Christ. Right now, Israel is waiting (3:4): then she shall be fully restored (3:5).

Let us summarize the analogy that develops through these chapters:

HOSEA AND GOMER	JEHOVAH AND ISRAEL
1. Hosea takes a wife who is pure.	1. Jehovah took Israel as a "chaste bride" at Mt. Sinai. He didn't take to Himself an idolatrous nation as a "wife," but a redeemed nation. Exodus 19.
2. Gomer bears *Hosea* a son, Jezreel (1:3).	2. Israel was fruitful to God at the beginning of the "marriage" (Jeremiah. 2:1-3) . . . No national idolatry or foreign alliances.
3. Gomer becomes unfaithful to Hosea (2:2-5) and has children by her lovers.	3. Israel became unfaithful as a nation: Calf and Baal worship evil alliances with nations (4-10).
4. Hosea separates from her (2:2).	4. God gave Israel up to her sins (2:6-13).
5. Gomer becomes enslaved to her lovers (2:5ff; 3:1-3).	5. Israel became enslaved to the Assyrians (one of her "lovers"), 2 Kings 15-17.
6. Hosea seeks Gomer out and delivers her from her slavery by paying the redemption price. Then he gives her a period of waiting before full restoration of marital rights (3:1-3).	6. Jehovah will deliver Israel some day and bring her to Himself. The redemption at Calvary is the basis for it, but Israel is waiting (3:4-5) for full restoration.

How God loves us! We have seen this dramatized in the life of Hosea and in the symbolism of the story. May this great, unfailing love of God which we have seen, and received, in Christ Jesus motivate us to a greater love for Him and others. May we be able to say with the apostle Paul: "THE LOVE OF CHRIST CONSTRAINS US . . ." (2 Corinthians 5:14).

Love is the greatest thing in the world. We are able to show love in our lives because God's love has been "shed abroad in our hearts by the Holy Spirit . . ." (Romans 5:5). Paul warns us that if we do not have love, we are nothing. The world around us needs love. Let us show that love where we are and to all with whom we associate.

II. THE UNFAILING LOVE OF GOD TO ISRAEL EXPOUNDED BY HOSEA IN SERMON FORM 4-14

One thing we observe in reading these prophetic sermons is that there is no time-element mentioned. Hosea did not date his sermons; we don't know for sure when he gave them. But this does not hinder us from understanding his message. These chapters "give in . . . detail what was set forth in broad outline and under the picture of a domestic scene in chapters one to three" (Feinberg). The messages include both kingdoms, but the Northern Kingdom is primarily in view.

A. GOD'S UNFAILING LOVE TO ISRAEL CANNOT COVER THEIR SIN, FOR GOD IS HOLY AND SIN MUST BE EXPOSED 4-8

Some have the idea that "love" allows anything and is tolerant of every kind of conduct. This is a purely worldly concept based on the philosophy of men. But God is not only love; He is holy and just. In His holiness, He has certain standards by which men are to live. He does not turn His head when these standards are violated. In His justice He requires punishment, without partiality, for the offender. God has been long-suffering with Israel, but this is not to be interpreted as approval of their life-style. He does not forget, and He requires that which is past unless there is repentance. The general flow of idea running through this section is: Israel is guilty of awful depravity (4-5:7) and thus is threatened with desolation unless they repent (5:8-7:7); their confidence in idols and foreign alliances will not save them (7:8-8:14).

1. THE AWFUL DEPRAVITY OF ISRAEL 4-5:7

The nation is rebuked for its inhumanity (4:1-3). The religious leaders of the nation (priests) are most responsible for this condition, for they have been unfaithful in teaching truth to the people (4:4-11). Their example has led the people into idolatry of the worst kind (4:12-19—cult-prostitution). Therefore, God will judge all (priests, king's house, and people) and no amount of animal sacrifice will atone for their depravity (5:1-7).

History confirms that, when a nation leaves the true knowledge of God for idols of their own making, all kinds of inhumanities are allowed and practiced—whether the idolatry is the worship of images, a philosophical system, or a political ideology. Communism and Nazism are modern day examples. *SATAN IS BEHIND IT ALL!!*

2. **THE ANTICIPATED DESOLATION OF ISRAEL** 5:8-7:7

Desolation will be the lot of Israel (and Judah, later) for their sin, and no foreign alliance (v. 13) can preserve them. The only hope for Israel lies in repentance (v. 15). Thus, Hosea challenges the nation, even at this eleventh hour, to return to the Lord and He will heal (6:1-3). The possibility of returning is unlikely for Israel is so chained in the spirit of whoredoms that any return might be, at best, superficial and short-lived (6:4-6). But what marvelous grace this is—that corrupt, rotten, depraved Israel (6:7-7:7) still has time to return. How heinous are the crimes, and how red-hot are the lusts from which these crimes proceed, but STILL GOD LOVES ISRAEL, Truly, "where sin abounded, grace did much more abound."

Are you bound by sin? Is there even a little determination to turn to God? Then do it now and He will receive you, no matter how low you have sunk!

3. **THE VAIN-CONFIDENCE OF ISRAEL** 7:8-8:14

Gomer was well-provided for by Hosea, but she wanted her lovers instead! So it was with Israel. God in His love had provided them with all that they needed, but they wanted their lovers instead. When they knew God, they glorified Him not as God neither were thankful, but became vain in their imaginations! Rather than trust the Lord with all their hearts, they leaned to their own understanding and cultivated the desires of their own hearts.

a. **The Vain-Confidence of Foreign Alliances** .... (7:8-8:14)

Did these nations help Israel? No, they "devoured its strength" (7:9). No wonder Hosea calls Israel "a cake not turned" (half-baked), and "a silly dove without heart (sense)" (7:8, 11). From one perspective, Israel was a prostitute who sold herself to the nations, but gained nothing from it. "What utter stupidity," we might say, but sin deceives the heart of man into doing the most outrageous and contradictory things.

The Scripture says, "Cursed is man that trusteth in man and maketh the flesh his arm" (Jeremiah 17:5). Believers who make alliances with the world should remember the words of James, "Whosoever . . . will be a friend of the world is the enemy of God (4:4). You cannot love the world and God at the same time. It is either God or the "present evil world." Paul said of a professing servant of Christ, "Demas has forsaken me, having loved this present world" (2 Timothy 4:10).

b.   The Vain-Confidence of Calf-Worship 8:5-14

Israel's corruption did not start with foreign alliances, but with the worship of the golden calves, instituted by Jeroboam I (1 Kings 12:25-33). Thus the root problem of Israel—"THY CALF, O SAMARIA . . ."—was an idol made by the hands of men (v. 6). How sad is the final verse of this chapter (v. 14): "FOR ISRAEL HATH FORGOTTEN HIS MAKER . . ."

B. GOD'S UNFAILING LOVE TO ISRAEL CANNOT PASS BY THEIR SIN FOR GOD IS JUST AND SIN MUST BE PUNISHED 9-10

Though Israel at the time of Hosea's prophesying was very wealthy and prosperous, they really had no reason for rejoicing (9:1-2). In spite of the good political, military and economic conditions of the Northern Kingdom the justice of God would in the not too distant future (722 BC) send the Northern Kingdom reeling into exile. The statement that Israel would return to *Egypt* (9:3, 6), is to be understood metaphorically of BONDAGE. Israel will return again to BONDAGE—this time in Assyria (9:3-6).

Wicked men hate the truth and they vent their anger on Hosea, calling him "a fool" and "mad" (9:7-8). But they deserve what's coming for they are just as corrupt as in the days of Gibeah (Judges. 19-21), and God will visit them with judgment (9:9).

As Hosea looks back to the early history of Israel in the wilderness, he speaks positively of the refreshment Israel was to God (grapes, figs), but it wasn't long before their idolatrous tendencies erupted in the event of Baal-peor. Numbers 22–25 give the background and story of this time (9:10). When the judgment of the exile comes, the Assyrian brutality and horrors will affect everyone—children as well as adults (9:11-13). This prospect causes Hosea great pain and fear; he cries out to God that the children may be spared the horrors to come by being cut off before entering life (9:14). Because of their wickedness (illustrated in the idol-shrine at Gilgal), they will be punished with exile and will wander among the nations (9:15-17).

Is there a lesson here for us? Do we misinterpret the times? Do we think that, because things are prosperous in our nation or in our lives, this necessarily means that God acknowledges our conduct as holy and righteous? We must measure our lives by the *Word of God,* not by the *blessing of God.* God often blesses the unrighteous because He wants to draw them to Himself by His love (compare Romans 2:1-5). O that Israel had estimated itself BY THE WORD! O that we might do this!

The more prosperous Israel became ("empty" in KJV is rendered "luxuriant" in NASV), the more they multiplied their idolatry (10:1). The very idols they worshiped will be carried off with them by the Assyrians, showing their impotence to protect; and the very places of worship will be destroyed (10:2-8a). Israel will not be able to escape this judgment when it is God's time to send it (8b-11). But Hosea still holds out hope for his corrupt people if they will only "seek" the Lord. WHAT GRACE! But if they will not return to the Lord, then destruction is certain (10:13-15).

Prosperity can be misinterpreted as God's stamp of approval on our conduct; it can also be a curse promoting self-sufficiency. Job was a man who had prosperity in balance (Job 1:1-5, 20-22). Paul warns of the dangers of prosperity (1 Timothy 6:8-10) and exhorts the prosperous to a right use of wealth (1 Timothy 6:17-19).

C. GOD IN HIS UNFAILING LOVE FOR ISRAEL WILL NOT GIVE THEM UP TO TOTAL DESTRUCTION FOR HE IS FAITHFUL TO HIS PROMISES 11-14

1. THE CHARACTER OF GOD'S FAITHFUL LOVE FOR ISRAEL 11:1-11

a. THE **COMPASSIONATE** LOVE OF THE FATHER 11:1-4

God is omnipotent and Israel is helpless. In His compassion and by His power He brought His helpless "child" out of slavery in Egypt. He saw His "son," Israel, in awful bondage and affliction (Exodus 2:23) and called him out of suffering. The Holy Spirit applies this verse to God's Son, Jesus Christ, who was also in Egypt for a time (Matthew 2:15). Israel's response to such compassionate love was not loving worship but a turning away to idols, even though the prophets pleaded with them (11:2). This action was completely unreasonable, for God had tenderly and patiently cared for Israel (11:3), and when Israel grew up as a nation God continued to love them, treating them in a humane way (11:4). How God loved Israel—compassionately—is how He loves us. Do we respond as Israel did?

b. THE **CHASTENING** LOVE OF THE FATHER 11:5-7

Solomon said, "My son, despise not the chastening of the LORD; . . . for *whom the Lord loveth* He correcteth . . ." (Proverbs 3:11-12). The Lord Jesus said, "Those whom I love, I reprove and discipline; be zealous therefore, and repent" (Revelation 3:19). If God hadn't loved Israel, He wouldn't have bothered about them, but because He loved this people, He must apply the pressure of chastisement. Here He threatens their subjection to the Assyrians and the destruction of their cities. The prophets tirelessly called

Israel to return to the "most High," but they would not exalt Him. If we are being chastened by our heavenly Father, is it because of our waywardness? Whatever the cause, let us cast ourselves upon Him and remember that if He did not love us, He wouldn't bother with us.

c. THE **COVENANT-LOVE** OF THE FATHER ... 11:8-11

What a heart-rending cry is the question of verse eight! "HOW SHALL I GIVE THEE UP, EPHRAIM?" God cannot give up His people, Israel, for He has an unconditional covenant with them. His covenant-love, which He has pledged to Israel, ensures that He will not totally destroy the nation or "execute the fierceness" of His anger toward them (11:8-9). In His love He will restore (11:10-11). Are we aware that God through Jesus Christ has a covenant-love for us? It is the New Covenant in Christ's blood. Christ has pledged to save and keep us in His love (Romans 8:31-39).

It should be observed that verse twelve of this chapter really goes with chapter twelve. In the Hebrew Scriptures 11:12 becomes 12:1, for it begins a new subject.

2. **THE CONFRONTATION OF GOD'S LOVE TO ISRAEL** 11:12-13:16

One modern-day Bible teacher has written that there are times when we need to be "caring enough to confront." The general idea is that if you love a person you will have to, at times, demonstrate that love in confrontation. Love confronts! Of course, love is creative and confronts in a multitude of ways. The way it confronts is, or should be, in keeping with the situation. In this section God confronted His people in two ways: *first*, by historical comparison—a contrast between Jacob the person and Jacob (Israel) the nation (11:12-12:14), and *second*, by emphasizing the consequences of sin—death (13).

a. **GOD IN HIS LOVE CONFRONTED ISRAEL FOR ITS FAITHLESSNESS BY WAY OF HISTORICAL COMPARISON** 11:12-12:14

There is no darker sin than to despise the love of God, but that is exactly what Israel did. God's love sought Israel's affection and trust but got only faithlessness in return. Israel, by their idolatry and foreign alliances with Egypt and Assyria, provoked the Lord to righteous anger. God is a jealous God and cannot tolerate any rivals to the devotion which He demands and deserves. In revealing Israel's faithlessness, by way of historical comparison, God appealed to their sense of reason. Logic and history would, or should, tell Israel the error of her way. Hosea contrasted the existing condition of Israel (Judah is brought in briefly) with the past fidelity of Israel's father, Jacob. How the nation has changed since then! This is NOT A CASE OF "LIKE FATHER, LIKE SON!" God exhorted His wayward people to return to Him (12:6).

(1) SINFUL ISRAEL AND JUDAH 11:12-12:2

Israel's whole national life was nothing but "lies" and "deceit." They carried on with this life-style while all the time claiming great religious devotion (11:12a). Judah was heading in the same direction, for they are accused of being unruly and wayward in the face of God's faithfulness (see 11:12b in the NASV. The Authorized Version is wrong in viewing Judah as faithful). Israel is feeding on a self-destroying diet by their alliances with the "east wind" (Assyria), and with Egypt. With great energy they pursue these alliances which will eventually bring their destruction (12:1). Chapter seventeen of 2 Kings gives the historical account of Assyria's destruction of the Northern Kingdom. Judah is no better than Israel and will reap what they sow (12:2).

(2) SPIRITUAL JACOB 12:3-6

The Picture 12:3-5

Hosea draws three episodes from the life of Jacob in which he is seen as energetically ambitious for spiritual things. Jacob had his failures, but Hosea emphasizes that which is commendable and worthy of emulation. In *infancy*, when he was coming out of the womb, he laid hold of Esau's heel, thus dramatizing his desire for the birthright (12:3a). In *manhood* he saw a vision of the Lord at Bethel

(12:4b-5). Then, as a much older adult, he wrestled with the angel of God and would not let go until he received the blessing of God (12:3b-4a). Yes, Jacob had his failures, like all of us, but unlike his brother Esau, he knew the value of God's blessings.

The Application 12:6

Israel needs to get back to the faith of their father, Jacob, so that it can be said of them, "LIKE FATHER, LIKE SON." But how? Hosea exhorts: "Therefore turn thou to thy God: keep mercy and judgment, and wait on thy God continually." There is to be genuine repentance, and there is to be the evidence of repentance which is morality, ethics, and daily trust in God. Are we like Jacob, ambitious for God's blessing? Paul says in 2 Corinthians 5:9: "We have as our ambition . . . to be pleasing to Him." Or are we like Israel—needing to get back to God in repentance, to straighten out our daily lives morally, ethically and spiritually, and to continually trust Him?

(3) SINFUL ISRAEL 12:7-11

If Israel should obey the exhortation of Hosea and come back to God, it would be phenomenal, for they have sunk to the depths of sin.

**SINFUL ISRAEL
CHARACTERIZED** 12:7-11

First, Self Degradation. "HE (Israel) is a *merchant,*" which means Israel is a CANAANITE! The word merchant comes from the same word translated Canaan in the O.T. (see your Bible margin). The Canaanites represented humanity in its most degraded form; the Jews had been commanded to destroy them as a judgment from God. Israel, instead of destroying them, left them in the land and became just like them—both in religion and in that which is emphasized in this verse, deceitful commercial practices. Happy is the man who does not condemn himself in that which he allows in his life! *Second, Self-Sufficiency.* Israel claimed that they had acquired all their riches on their own. Arrogance and self-sufficiency are brothers (12:8a)! *Third, Self-Deception.* Israel is so deceived that they do not know their own condition (12:8b). There is no worse state than to be self-deceived. Conscience no longer functions as a moral and ethical indicator, and evil becomes holiness in the eyes of the sinner. Isaiah warned: "Woe unto them that call evil good and good evil!" The apostle John said, "If we say that we have no sin, we deceive ourselves, and the truth is not in us" (1 John 1:8).

SINFUL ISRAEL THREATENED 12:9

Though Assyria will do the chastening, it comes from God—their God who redeemed them from Egypt. The chastisement will be for them "to dwell in tabernacles (tents), as in the days of the solemn feast." In other words, when the Assyrians come into their land and destroy their cities and take them off to captivity, they will go back to living in tents as they lived in the wilderness for forty years before coming into the land.

SINFUL ISRAEL UNEXCUSED 12:10-11

On the one hand, when the chastisement comes, Israel cannot claim *IGNORANCE* for they know God's will. The prophets have spoken to Israel many times in many ways as to what the Lord requires from His people (v. 10). Nor, on the other hand, can Israel claim *INNOCENCE*, for the evidence of their idolatry abounds, as represented by Gilead on the east of Jordan and Gilgal on the west. The mention of Gilgal brings back many memories, for it was the first place the nation encamped after crossing Jordan. It was in Gilgal that Israel was circumcised after being 40 years in the wilderness. It was there that they celebrated the passover, and it was from there that they began their conquest of Palestine under Joshua (Joshua 5). But now Gilgal is known for its idolatry! What a shame!

As we look back over our lives, do we remember the Gilgal of our consecration? Is it the same today, or do we say about ourselves, "What a shame"?

(4) SPIRITUAL JACOB 12:12-13

Hosea switches back to Jacob. Jacob had to flee to Mesopotamia. While at his uncle Laban's, he was oppressed and made to serve like the lowest of servants, but this did not turn him away from the Lord (Romans 5:3-4) for he clung to the promises given him at Bethel (Genesis 28:15). What an example of enduring hardship! When he returned to the promised land, he continued to live the life of faith! But what about Israel? After having been delivered from Egypt by a prophet (Moses), and after having been guarded by Moses (12-13), what did Israel do? They provoked God to bitter anger (12:14).

b. GOD IN HIS LOVE CONFRONTED ISRAEL FOR ITS FAITHLESSNESS BY WAY OF EMPHASIS ON THE CONSEQUENCES OF SIN—DEATH 13

This chapter should be read in the NASV for a clearer understanding of its contents. It is a very sad commentary on the depths to which Israel has sunk, showing the judgment God must bring.

The Bible says that "the wages of sin is death." This chapter is a graphic illustration of that truth. Here we see the death of the Northern Kingdom of Israel both *RELIGIOUSLY* and *NATIONALLY*. The *RELIGIOUS* death of the nation is described in terms of the past (13:1-8). The *NATIONAL* death of the nation is described in terms of the future— prophetically predicted (13:9-16).

(1) THE DEATH OF THE NATION RELIGIOUSLY 13:1-8

IDOLATRY 13:1-3

The prophet Hosea, in order to show how far Israel has sunk in idolatrous apostasy, points to the beginning of the Northern Kingdom (13:1a). God promised to the first king, Jeroboam I, prosperity and an enduring kingdom if he obeyed His commandments (1 Kings 11:37,38). But Jeroboam almost immediately introduced calf worship to the Northern Ten Tribes (1 Kings 12:28-30). Baal worship came a little later in the reign of wicked King Ahab (1 Kings 16:29-33). The increase in idolatry in the Northern Kingdom was a manifestation of Israel's spiritual death. Such idolatry would bring swift destruction (13:3).

INGRATITUDE 13:4-6

God's goodness was manifested when He came into covenant relationship with Israel and He had faithfully cared for Israel ever since the covenant relationship was established. But what thanks did He get? Israel became self-satisfied, arrogant, and forgetful of God. How sad! Israel took God for granted and exalted themselves! How easy it is to slip into the sin of ingratitude. It is the tendency of our human nature to be selfish and forget the source of our blessings.

THE PREDICTION OF THE JUDGMENT 13:7-8

The judgment will be *FEROCIOUS* (13:7-8). God likens Himself to wild beasts who lurk for the prey, pounce on it, and tear it to pieces, devouring it in the process. What an awful picture of severe judgment. It should make one tremble!

(2) THE DEATH OF ISRAEL, NATIONALLY 13:9-16

It is the religious death of the nation that makes way for its national death. God will rip Israel, the Northern Kingdom, from its land and carry away the nation to Assyria. The Southern Kingdom would experience a similar fate much later on in its history.

When the judgment comes, it will be *INESCAPABLE* (13:9-11). It doesn't pay to be against God. No king will be able to save Israel when God smites the nation. Israel should reflect on her history and take note that God gave her kings in his anger and took them away in His wrath.

The judgment is *JUST*. God has not disregarded Israel's sin. They cannot plead innocence. No! Their guilt has been carefully treasured and their sin safely stored away.

They will not get away with it (13:12). The judgment is *NEAR,* but Israel could still repent and be born anew. On the one hand, Israel is likened to a woman suffering the pains of childbirth. God has been afflicting Israel with the pain of chastisement and these pains are reminders of their being delivered up to the Assyrians. On the other hand, Israel is likened to a child that is almost ready to be born but gets stalled in the birth canal. Unless the child comes to birth there will be death. So with Israel. They are in the valley of decision. If they do not repent and be born anew they will experience certain death, *nationally*—being taken into captivity. God says, Israel is "not a wise son." He is just an inch away from life, but has chosen death (13:13).

In the midst of this darkness of national destruction comes a ray of hope (13:14), for the message of judgment is accompanied by a message of *PROMISE OF REDEMPTION.* Hosea envisioned a time when the religiously and nationally dead nation would come to life again. This promise is yet to be fulfilled. The apostle Paul took this up in 1 Corinthians 15 and applied it to the victory over physical death that each believer in Jesus Christ would experience. Death and Sheol will not win out ultimately. The judgment, when it comes, will be *BRUTAL* (13:15-16). Assyria will come in mighty destructive power to plunder, multilate and kill.

3. THE PROSPECTS OF GOD'S FAITHFUL LOVE TO ISRAEL—RESTORATION 14

God has not finished with Israel. He has committed Himself to this nation and will not revoke His promises (Romans 11:29).

a. THE PRE-REQUISITE TO RESTORATION— "Return" 14:1-3

Hosea uses the term "return" several times in his prophecy. Sometimes it has to do with God's call to Israel to repent. That is how it is used here. Let us observe things about this challenge to "return."

(1) Who Is to Return?—"Return, *O ISRAEL* . . ." 14:1a

"Israel" stands for the Northern Kingdom. In verse eight the Northern Kingdom is called "Ephraim."

(2) Where Is Israel to Return?—"to the Lord your God" 14:1b

Hosea does not call them to return to religion. They have plenty of that. Turning to religion would not require repentance! It is only turning to the Lord that will insure that the Lord will restore them to blessing (Zechariah 1:3; Joel 2:12).

(3) Why Should Israel Return? 14:1c,3

First, because they have "fallen" ("stumbled" in NASV) by their iniquity. This fall has left them in jeapordy of judgment (14:1c).

Second, because all the things they trusted will not save them from the prophesied destruction of the Northern Kingdom. Their foreign alliances with Assyria and Egypt (where they got their "horses"), and their worship of the idols of their own making will be of no help. Israel is like a helpless orphan child. Only the Lord can save Israel from judgment (14:3).

(4) How Should Israel Return—14:2

They are to "take . . . words" and return to the Lord. Animal sacrifice will be of no avail. What God wants is the true confession of sin from the heart. If they are willing to genuinely comply, the Lord will take away their sin and receive them graciously. Forgiveness is based on *grace* not merit.

b. THE RESULTS OF RESTORATION 14:4-8

(1) Healing—"I will heal their backsliding." 14:4a

Israel as a nation has had the disease of spiritual apostasy. God, upon their repentance, will cure them.

(2) Love—"I will love them freely" 14:4b

To be loved "freely" means that God will love them without restruction or reservation. Sin hinders the full expression of love. This is very true in the realm of human love in any variety of human relationships.

(3) Prosperity 14:5-7

The Cause of Prosperity—"*I will be* like the dew to Israel" 14:5a.

The dew refreshes the ground so that it might prosper physically. The Lord will refresh Israel spiritually so that the nation may be prosperous.

The Description of the Prosperity 14:5b-7

Many similes are used to describe the various aspects of the prosperity which Israel will enjoy. "He will blossom *like* the lily, and he will take root *like* the cedars of Lebanon. His shoots will sprout, and his beauty will be *like* the olive tree, and his fragrance *like* the cedars of Lebanon. Those who live in his shadow will again raise grain, and they will blossom *like* the vine. His renown will be *like* the wine of Lebanon." These similes bring out the *character, fruitfulness* and *influence* of the restored nation. They picture Israel in the future day as being abundantly fruitful toward God, nationally stable, manifesting the signs of true spiritual life, the attractive nation among the Gentiles that God always wanted it to be, having an admirable lifestyle, being a blessing to the nations and having a world-wide influence for good.

These similes have their parallel in the life of the Christian. God is seeking to shape our character (Romans 12:1-2), produce spiritual fruit in and through us (John 15; Galatians 5:22, 23), and make us a dynamic influence in the earth (Matthew 28:18-20).

(4) Reminder and Warning—14:8-9

The *reminder* is a loving reminder. God asks the question, "O Ephraim, what more have I to do with idols?" This is just another way of saying, "I have had enough of your Idolatry!" Israel only needs God. The Lord said, "It is I who answer and look after you." It is God, not idols, who answers Israel's prayers and provides for them. To enforce his point, God said, "I am like a luxuriant cypress; From Me comes your fruit."

In likening Himself to a "luxuriant cypress" he is simply saying that He is sufficient for all Israel's needs. They need no other help. He has all the resources they need.

It must be noted that some Bible students see 14:8 as a dialogue between the nation and God. Ephraim (Israel) speaks and God answers. Ephraim speaks again and God responds. Note the breakdown (based on the KJV).

Ephraim: "Ephraim shall say, What have I to do anymore with idols?"

God: "I have heard him, and observed him."

Ephraim: "I am like a green fir tree."

God: "From me is thy fruit found."

In this view, Ephraim's commitment is that she is through with idolatry. She has learned her lesson and renounces it. God hears and observes this commitment and looks with favor on Israel's renunciation of idolatry. Ephraim responds, "I am like a green fir (cypress) tree." This boast appears to be presumptuous, however. God then reminds Israel that her fruit is from Him, not gained on her own.

The lesson to be gained from this particular view of verse 8 is that when we have commited ourselves to the Lord and He begins to prosper our lives, there is always the danger of taking on feelings of self-sufficiency. We need to constantly remind ourselves that everything we have is from Him. This will keep us humble and trusting.

The loving reminder merges with a loving *warning* (14:9): "Whoever is wise, let him understand these things; Whoever is discerning, let him know them. For the ways of the LORD are right, And the righteous will walk in them, But transgressors will stumble in them."

This verse is like many found in the book of Proverbs. There are just two paths in life: the way of the righteous and the way of the transgressors. The first leads to blessing, but the other to castastrophe and judgment. We know which way Israel has been taking. On which path are you? If you are wise and discerning, you will know and understand the message Hosea has been unfolding throughout these fourteen chapters.

6

The Book of Micah

What do you think of first when the prophet Micah comes to mind? That's right, the birthplace of Jesus: "BUT THOU, BETHLEHEM EPHRATHAH, THOUGH THOU BE LITTLE AMONG THE THOUSANDS OF JUDAH, YET OUT OF THEE SHALL HE COME FORTH UNTO ME THAT IS TO BE RULER IN ISRAEL; WHOSE GOINGS FORTH HAVE BEEN FROM OF OLD, FROM EVERLASTING" (Micah 5:2; cp. Matthew 2:5-6). Isaiah revealed the nature of Christ's birth (virgin born); Micah was the only prophet to reveal the place of His birth—Bethlehem in Judah. This is marvellous, indeed, but unfortunately this is about all that many believers know about this fascinating book. There is much, much more to learn and appreciate. May this lesson stimulate your interest to study this great prophecy in detail.

I. THE MAN, MICAH

A. HIS NAME

There are some people who hate their own names. Some dislike them to the extent that they legally change them. Any one in Israel with the name Micah (there were seven Micahs mentioned in the Old Testament) would have been proud to bear that name for it means "WHO IS LIKE JEHOVAH." Micah is a shortened form of Micaiah (just as Jim is a short form of James), and there is a play on this name in 7:18: "WHO IS A GOD LIKE UNTO THEE, THAT PARDONETH INIQUITY . . ." Israel needs pardon and God is ready to extend it to them if they repent.

B. HIS PERSONAL HISTORY

We know much of the personal history of other prophets, but next to nothing about Micah. In fact, the only thing we can say is that he was a Morasthite from the town of Moresheth. This village was situated about twenty miles southwest of Jerusalem and was very near Gath in northern Philistia. It was not far from the famous city of Lachish, and was close to the international highway that ran from Mesopotamia to Egypt.

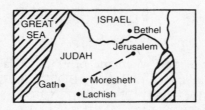

C. HIS MINISTRY

1. THE TIME OF HIS MINISTRY

a. GENERALLY, DURING THE REIGNS OF JOTHAM, AHAZ AND HEZEKIAH

Chapter one, verse one reads: "THE WORD OF THE LORD THAT CAME TO MICAH THE MORASTHITE IN THE DAYS OF *JOTHAM, AHAZ* AND *HEZEKIAH* KINGS OF JUDAH . . ." (1:1a). See your chart once again. Jotham and Hezekiah were good kings, but Ahaz was very evil. He made an alliance with Assyria and was a promoter of idolatry. Micah was an eighth century prophet along with Amos, Hosea and Isaiah. He had much in common with Amos which we will see later.

b. SPECIFICALLY, IT IS DIFFICULT TO DETERMINE WITH PRECISION

We know that his ministry began before 722 BC, for he prophesies the destruction of the Northern Kingdom by the Assyrians, which took place in that year (1:5-9a). But just where in Jotham's reign he began his ministry, and how far into Hezekiah's reign he prophesied, we do not know with certainty. Scholars estimate that Micah began to prophesy in the latter part of Jotham's kingship (738 BC) and continued until the middle of Hezekiah's reign (698 BC).

2. THE INTERNATIONAL SETTING OF HIS MINISTRY

The *Syrian empire* which God has used as a chastening instrument against the Northern Kingdom, Israel, is weak and about to fall. The *Assyrian empire* is the power to be reckoned with. Syria will be destroyed by the Assyrians in 732 BC, and ten years later Israel will fall to this mighty power. God not only uses *nature* (Joel 1-2) but He uses *nations* to correct and punish His erring children.

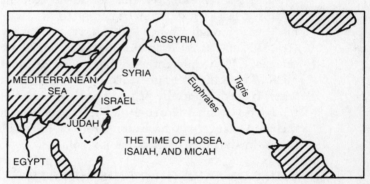

The Northern Kingdom is on the brink of disaster, and the Southern Kingdom is politically, religiously, morally and spiritually sick (see Isaiah 1).

3. THE PLACE OF HIS MINISTRY

Micah evidently did his prophesying in Jerusalem. This was a case of the small town boy coming to the big city. In Jerusalem he preached against the two kingdoms in general, and specifically against the wealthy land-grabbers, leaders, prophets and priests (2-3). Jeremiah mentions Micah's ministry to Hezekiah and the people of his reign (Jeremiah 26:16-19).

4. **THE POWER OF HIS MINISTRY**

Micah confessed, "BUT TRULY I AM FULL OF POWER BY THE SPIRIT OF THE LORD . . ." (3:8). This power was evidenced in his fearless preaching to "DECLARE UNTO JACOB HIS TRANSGRESSION, AND TO ISRAEL HIS SIN" (3:8b). We need Spirit-empowered preaching in our day and age. Much preaching today just tickles the ear and puffs up the people—sparing the preacher from any negative criticism. Phillips paraphrases 2:11: "THE SORT OF PROPHET THIS PEOPLE WANTS IS A WINDBAG AND A LIAR, . . ."

5. **THE EFFECT OF HIS MINISTRY**

Nothing is said of the effect of Micah's ministry on Jotham and Ahaz. It is clear, however, that it had no influence on Ahaz because he was wicked from beginning to end, as evidenced by his unwise foreign alliance with Assyria and his gross idolatry (read 2 Kings 16, 2 Chronicles 28, and Isaiah 7 for background on Ahaz). How different was Ahaz's son, Hezekiah! This was NOT a case of "like father, like son." Jeremiah tells us that when Hezekiah and the people heard Micah's ministry, they repented (Jeremiah 26:16-19). There have been many godly men and women who have come from UNGODLY homes. It is only by the grace of God that it is so!

6. **THE COMPARISON OF HIS MINISTRY WITH THAT OF AMOS**

Micah and Amos have much in common. They were both from small towns but preached in a big city; both were imbued with a sense of the justice and judgment of God; both were fearless in their preaching; both emphasized the necessity of sincere religion; both were defenders of the lot of the poor; both rebuked the sinful leadership of the nation; both revealed the coming Messianic age—however, Micah spoke more about this than Amos. If they should preach in our modern day pulpits, we might feel mighty uncomfortable with their searing, blazing, straightforward ministry.

II. THE BOOK OF MICAH

A. THE THEME OF THE BOOK

The theme of Micah is generally typical of the Old Testament prophets. It is *THE JUDGMENT AND KINGDOM OF GOD.* This theme is developed in three major sections. The first section (1-3) announces judgment on the divided kingdom, generally (1), and then proceeds to denounce men of wealth and position in particular (2-3). The second section deals with the yet-future KING AND KINGDOM OF GOD IN CONTRAST TO PAST JUDGMENT AND CAPTIVITY (4-5). The last section deals primarily with judgment, but is different in *FORM* from the first two. It is in the form of a court-case. Jehovah is judge, Micah is the prosecuting attorney, creation is both witness and jury, and Israel is the defendant. The judge has a "controversy" (complaint, lawsuit) against His people (6-7). They are guilty, but there is yet hope. Micah, like so many of the prophets, ends on a very positive and wonderful note (7:18-20).

B. THE STYLE OF THE BOOK

Scholars tell us that from the standpoint of language and writing Micah possessed great literary ability. Interestingly enough, he uses the artistic device known as the "pun" in 1:10-16. A pun is a play on words. J.B. Phillips seeks to bring out this literary form with clarity. Note just a sample (1:10-11):

> "So then, in *GATH* where tales are told, *breathe not a word!*
> In *ACCO*, the town of Weeping, *shed no tear!*
> In *APHRAH*, the house of Dust, *grovel in the dust!*
> And you who live in *SHAPHIR*, the beauty town, move on, *for your shame lies naked!*
> You who live in *ZAANAN*, the town of march, *there is no marching for you now!*
> And *BETH-EZEL*, standing on the hillside, *can give no foothold in her sorrow.*"

The most interesting play on names is that of his own, as seen in 7:18.

OUTLINE OF THE BOOK

The outline follows the theme, THE JUDGMENT AND KINGDOM OF GOD.

I. THE COMING JUDGMENT OF GOD 1-3

A. GENERALLY, THE JUDGMENT UPON THE DIVIDED KINGDOM 1

The *CALL* to Judgment (1:1-4) is followed by the *CAUSE* (1:5) and *SEVERITY* of the Judgment (1:6-16). The cause is stated to be "the transgression of Jacob" and the "sins of the house of Israel." The severity is such that the Northern Kingdom (represented by its capital, Samaria) will be totally destroyed, (1:6-9a), while the Southern Kingdom, Judah, will lose many of its cities and find the Assyrian invader right at the gates of Jerusalem (1:9b-16). The destruction of the Northern Kingdom was accomplished in 722 BC. The subjection of the Southern Kingdom referred to in 1:9b-16 took place in 701 BC at the hands of Sennacherib, King of Assyria, who ruled from 705 to 681 BC. See 2 Kings 18-20 for background of the Assyrian invasion of Judah.

B. SPECIFICALLY, THE JUDGMENT UPON MEN OF POWER AND INFLUENCE 2-3

Micah did not try to curry favor with the "powers that be." He was no respector of persons! He said what needed to be spoken, showing no favoritism. He first of all *CONDEMNS MEN OF WEALTH* (2). Not all wealthy men are unrighteous. Some men of wealth have been greatly used of God. Micah is not condemning the possession of wealth, but the *motivation* and *ways* by which it is obtained (2:1-2). These men will reap what they have sown (2:3-5). Of course, they don't want Micah to preach this kind of message to them (2:6-7), but because of their inhuman treatment of the poor (2:8-10), and the compromising of other prophets who are windbags and materialists (2:11), he cannot hold his tongue. The chapter closes on a note of hope, which would be especially precious to the downtrodden and oppressed. It refers to the Messiah and His chosen remnant (2:12-13).

From men of wealth he turns to rebuke *MEN OF POSITION AND LEADERSHIP* (3). The rulers (3:1-4) are butchers, devouring the people; the prophets (vv. 5-7) and the priests (v. 11) all minister for money. Micah, empowered by the Spirit to speak (3:8), condemns these men and their practices and *prophesies the coming destruction of Jerusalem* (3:9-12). The leaders should have been self-sacrificing shepherds of the flock (nation), but they were greedy and selfish. How this should speak to leaders of God's people in any age! What motivates us to be in positions of power and leadership? Are we interested in our paycheck, or in the edification and upbuilding of the people of God? Did the leaders repent? Did the Lord destroy Jerusalem (3:12)? We have evidence from the book of Jeremiah that King Hezekiah and the people repented—and God spared the city (Jeremiah 26:18-19). If our motives and ambitions for serving God's people are not sanctified, then we need to do what Hezekiah and the people did—REPENT!

II. THE FUTURE KINGDOM AND KING IN CONTRAST WITH THE PAST 4-5

Though the kindgom of the past failed and ultimately was destroyed through invasions and captivities, God consistently holds out the unconditional promise of a glorious kingdom over which His beloved Son, Jesus Christ, shall rule. In this section the future kingdom is contrasted with the past. There are many abrupt changes throughout this section; it switches back and forth between the past and the future.

A. THE KINGDOM 4-5:1

1. THE KINGDOM OF THE FUTURE DESCRIBED 4:1-8

The *CENTER* of the Kingdom will be Mt. Zion (4:1). Included in its *CITIZENSHIP* are the nations (see Matthew 25:34) who trusted in Jesus during the Tribulation Period (4:2a). What gives significance to the coming Kingdom is the fact that its *CHIEF ADMINISTRATOR* is the Lord (4:2b-3a) who will *teach* His law and *judge* among the nations. Because the Lord is King, the Kingdom will be *CHARACTERIZED* by peace (v. 3b), security (v. 4), and holiness (v. 5, NASV). the *CHIEF NATION* of the Kingdom will be restored Israel, who in the past has been greatly afflicted (v. 6), but in that future day will be a strong nation (vv. 7, 8).

There is inscribed on one of the walls of the United Nations building in New York City part of Micah 4:3: *"AND THEY SHALL BEAT THEIR SWORDS INTO PLOWSHARES AND THEIR SPEARS INTO PRUNINGHOOKS: NATION SHALL NOT LIFT UP A SWORD AGAINST NATION, NEITHER SHALL THEY LEARN WAR ANY MORE."* In other words, it is the goal and hope of this world organization that there will come a time when war is obliterated and people will forever live in peace. How unfortunate that the entirety of Micah 4:3 was not quoted! For without it, the realization of the United Nations' motto cannot be accomplished! It is because the Lord *"shall judge among many people, and rebuke strong nations afar off"* that this motto will some day be fulfilled! He is the PRINCE OF PEACE, and some day the "GOVERNMENT SHALL BE UPON HIS SHOULDER" (Isaiah 9:6).

2. THE KINGDOM OF THE PAST TO BE CHASTIZED 4:9-10

Israel will be restored some day as God's redeemed remnant, but before this happens, Micah reveals that they will be punished by captivity in Babylon. This captivity took place in three deportations to Babylon from 605 BC to 586 BC when the ancient city of Jerusalem was destroyed. From this 70-year captivity God would deliver His people.

3. THE KINGDOM OF THE FUTURE WILL BE TRIUMPHANT 4:11-13

In that coming day when Israel shall be triumphant, the Lord will use His nation to achieve the victory. Zechariah, chapters 12–14, has much to say about this aspect of future triumph. Observe the imagery used in verse thirteen of Israel as God's instrument of victory.

4. THE KINGDOM OF THE PAST TO BE CHASTIZED 5:1

When the chastisement of Judah takes place, the city of Jerusalem will be besieged and captured, and its judge (that is, king) will be punished ("they shall smite the judge of Israel with a rod upon the cheek"). This verse, in the Hebrew Bible, belongs at the end of chapter four.

B. THE KING—Jesus Christ 5:2-15

1. HIS FIRST ADVENT 5:2-3

The *PLACE OF HIS ADVENT* was the very small village of Bethlehem in Judah. To this very day, thousands make pilgrimages to this small town, much bigger now than then, to see the place where the incarnate Son of God stepped out of eternity into time (2a).

> "Down from His glory, came God's Son in lowly grace,
> To tell love's story and redeem the race. O the glorious
> mystery of the Babe in Bethlehem, Great event of history,
> God becoming man."

The first ones to seek the Christ in Bethlehem were lowly shepherds (Luke 2). Then came the visit of the Wise Men (Matthew 2). They all went to worship Him.

The *PURPOSE OF HIS ADVENT* was to rule (v. 2b). However, "He came unto His own and His own received Him not" John 1:12. They said they would not have this man to reign over them. Some day this rejected One shall fulfill that for which He came: "JESUS SHALL REIGN WHERE'ER THE SUN DOTH ITS SUCCESSIVE JOURNEYS RUN."

This One born in lowly Bethlehem did not have His beginnings there for He was *PRE-EXISTENT TO HIS ADVENT* (v. 2c). His "goings forth have been from of old, from everlasting." This one who lived only 33 years on earth is the ETERNAL SON OF GOD! "Great is the mystery of godliness, GOD MANIFEST IN THE FLESH" (1 Timothy 3:16).

Verse three refers to the *PERIOD BETWEEN THE ADVENTS* when Israel would be in affliction throughout the world (v. 3). That period is in process right now.

2.   **HIS SECOND ADVENT** 5:4-15

Hundreds of times in the Old Testament the Second Coming of Jesus Christ to earth is prophesied. The Second Coming is to be distinguished from the Rapture of the church. The church will be caught up to meet the Lord Jesus *in the air* (1 Thessalonians 4:13-18). Then there will be seven years of tribulation on the earth (Rev. 4-18). After this, the Lord Jesus will come back to earth to put down all other rule and authority and to reign over the earth for 1,000 years (Revelation 19:11-20:10).

a.   **THE NATURE OF HIS RULE WHEN HE COMES** 5:4a

What a beautiful picture! At His advent, He will be to His people all that the Jewish kings before Him on the throne of David should have been. He will tenderly "feed" (shepherd) His people.

b.   **THE RESULT OF HIS RULE WHEN HE COMES** 5:4b-15

Note the marvellous results of His Second Advent to the earth: (1) He shall be great throughout the earth (5:4b); (2) He shall *"be the peace"* when He comes. (This clause should be placed not with verse five, but at the end of verse four.) He not only shall bring peace, but He shall "BE THE PEACE"; (3) He shall protect His people from the "Assyrian" (5:5-6), referring to the future invader from the North who will try to destroy Israel; (4) He shall establish His long-awaited Kingdom in the earth, spoken of in 4:1-8 (5:7-15). When this happens, Israel will be a blessing to the world ("dew"— v. 7), chief over the nations ("lion"—v. 8), safe from her enemies ("enemies shall be cut off"—v. 9), and she will be totally trusting in the Lord. Everything they trusted in formerly will be "cut off" (vv. 10-15). WHAT A DAY THAT SHALL BE! Can you imagine what it will be like when Jesus has His rightful place in the earth?

"Our Lord is still rejected and by the world disowned,
By the many still neglected, and by the few enthroned.
But soon He'll come in glory; the hour is drawing nigh.
The crowning day is coming, by and by."

When Jesus comes back to earth, the church which had been raptured seven years before, will come with Him (1 Thessalonians 3:13) and will reign with Him. What a glorious future awaits us!

III. GOD'S LAWSUIT AGAINST HIS PEOPLE ISRAEL 6-7

We have already mentioned that this section is quite different in form from the first five chapters. Refer to previous comments in regard to this.

A. MICAH, THE PROSECUTOR, CALLS THE COURT TO ORDER 6:1a

"Hear now what the Lord is saying . . ."

B. GOD, THE JUDGE, GIVES CHARGE TO MICAH TO PLEAD HIS CAUSE 6:1b

"Arise, contend thou before the mountains, and let the hills hear thy voice."

C. MICAH, THE PROSECUTOR, MAKES HIS OPENING REMARKS TO THE JURY 6:2

Creation is both jury and witness of the sin of God's people.

D. GOD, THE JUDGE, ISSUES HIS COMPLAINT AGAINST THE DEFENDANT, ISRAEL 6:3-5

As the Lord issues His complaint, there are no words of harsh denunciation or judgment, rather the lament of a heartbroken Father over the waywardness of His child: "O my people, what have I done unto thee? and wherein have I wearied thee? testify against me" (v. 3). The Lord has only done good to Israel—delivering them from Egypt's bondage, giving them a gifted and dedicated leadership (v. 4), and preserving them from annihilation in the wilderness by Balak and Balaam (v. 5). Bringing these things to Israel's remembrance should speak to their conscience. In the light of these kindnesses they have been evil in their conduct. How quickly we forget God's goodness to us and go on our selfish ways!

E. THE DEFENDANT, ISRAEL, RESPONDS TO THE COMPLAINT 6:6-7

Israel's reponse is typical of any religious person who thinks that the sum and substance of religion is church ritual. Many think that going to church and taking part in the ritual of the service is all that God requires. Israel's response is: "Haven't we been religious? Haven't we brought sacrifices as Jehovah prescribed? What more does the Lord require of us?"

F. MICAH, THE PROSECUTOR, ANSWERS ISRAEL'S DEFENSE 6:8-9

Micah says, "Israel, you aren't ignorant of what God requires. You know that religion without ethics and morals is empty and meaningless. The Lord requires justice, loving kindness, and humility." Israel professes to know God: their life-style should evidence this relationship. The poet has said, "WHAT YOU *ARE* SPEAKS SO LOUDLY THAT THE WORLD CAN'T HEAR WHAT YOU *SAY*. THEY'RE LOOKING AT YOUR *WALK*, NOT LISTENING TO YOUR *TALK*." The man of wisdom (v. 9) will take heed and fear the Lord.

G. GOD, THE JUDGE, DECLARES THE DEFENDANT GUILTY AND ANNOUNCES ISRAEL'S PUNISHMENT 6:10-16

Israel's "treasures of wickedness", their unethical business practices (6:10-12), their apostasy in forsaking Jehovah for Baal ("status of Omri," v. 16) will bring stiff chastisement (6:13-15). Any professing worshiper of the Lord who persists in sin will not go unpunished.

H. THE DEFENDANT, ISRAEL, RESPONDS TO THE JUDGE'S INDICTMENT 7

1. CONFESSION OF GUILT 7:1-6

The only way to repent toward God is to plead guilty with a sincere heart. Israel bewails her moral corruption in society in general (7:1-2), in high places (7:3-4), and in family life

(7:5-6). Violence, corruption among leaders, betrayal of confidence in so close a relationship as family life are confessed. "If we confess our sins, he is faithful and just to forgive us our sins, and to cleanse us from all unrighteousness" (1 John 1:9).

2.   **EXPRESSION OF CONFIDENCE** 7:7-13

How beautiful are these verses. In the midst of the darkness, the nation expresses *FAITH*, "I will look unto the Lord"; *PATIENCE*, "I will wait for the God of my salvation"; and *HOPE*, "my God will hear me!" The last confidence, *HOPE*, is emphasized in verses 8-13. The indignation that they will experience at the hands of their enemies, as directed by the Lord, will be reversed. Their enemies may gloat over them, but the tables will be turned and the situation will be reversed, for Israel will be restored and her enemies will be ashamed.

3.   **PETITION FOR RESTORATION** 7:14-20

The *request is made* that God would intervene in their behalf "as in the days of old" (v. 14). In those days, He supernaturally worked for them. The *answer is then given* that God will indeed manifest His mighty power in their behalf just as in the days when He brought His people out of Egypt. Then the nations were amazed; so in the future day of deliverance the nations will be astounded and afraid (vv. 15-17). In view of such a wonderful answer Micah closes his prophecy with a *doxology of praise* (7:18-20) in which he extolls the excellency of our God: "WHO IS A GOD LIKE UNTO THEE?" The answer is, THERE IS NO GOD COMPARABLE TO JEHOVAH, the ONLY TRUE GOD!

Three excellencies of the Lord are then elaborated: His Forgiving Love (v. 18), His Redeeming power (v. 19), and His Unfailing Faithfulness (v. 20).

The book of Micah began with a picture of Jehovah coming to judge, and ends with Jehovah coming to bless. Have you noticed how so many of the prophets give us the BAD NEWS FIRST, and then relate THE GOOD NEWS? Even in the darkest hour there is the shining of hope.

7

The Book of Nahum

An amazing thing happened in the middle of the nineteenth century, AD. A city that had disappeared from history for hundreds and hundreds of years was re-discovered. It was the ancient city of Nineveh, the capital of the Assyrian empire. In 612 BC, this famous city on the Tigris River was so completely destroyed that it seemed in succeeding centuries like a mythical city until it was re-discovered by Austen Layard and others. The city has now been carefully excavated and has yielded many fine treasurers which aid in understanding history. Its ruins stand as mute testimony to the fact that the nation that forgets God will be turned into hell (Psalm 9:17). But did this nation really know God so that it could "forget" Him? Absolutely! Do you not recall that Jonah had gone to Nineveh in the eighth century BC during the time of Jeroboam II's kingship over the Northern Kingdom? Do you not remember that when he preached God's message of judgment to Nineveh, the whole city repented (Jonah 3)? Yes, they knew God then in a personal way, but after the passing of one hundred and fifty years or more, in Nahum's time, Nineveh was back to its old ways and had become as vicious, cruel and corrupt as in the days of Jonah! Yes, a lot can happen in a hundred and fifty years, and this time Nineveh is so far gone that they are past the possibility of repentance. There is now no hope for Nineveh as Nahum lashes out against this imperialistic, despotic pagan nation that found its modern counterpart in the barbarism of Nazi Germany. O how Nineveh has raped the nations! Their judgment will be total obliteration!

I. NAHUM, THE MAN

A. HIS NAME

This prophet is the only one mentioned in the Old Testament with this name. It means COMFORT or CONSOLATION. Though his message is one of unrelieved doom for Nineveh, it would bring untold COMFORT and CONSOLATION to those nations oppressed by Nineveh—especially to Judah (1:15) which at this point is the only Jewish kingdom left. The Northern Kingdom had already been destroyed by the Assyrians in 722 BC.

B. HIS PERSONAL HISTORY

We know nothing of the personal history of Nahum. In this regard, he resembles Obadiah, Micah, etc., and, as we have said before, this in no way affects our understanding of his prophecy.

C. HIS HOMETOWN

The first verse of chapter one declares that Nahum was "the Elkoshite." He was from the town of Elkosh. The locality of this village has always been a subject of debate among scholars. Note some of these views:

1.   That Elkosh is really the village of Caper*NAUM*. Capernaum means *the village of Nahum*. Capernaum was in the Northern Kingdom.

2.   That Elkosh is to be identified with the village of AL-KUSH which is approximately 25 miles north of ancient Nineveh (on the left bank of the Tigris river where his tomb is allegedly located).

3.   That Elkosh is to be identified with Elcesei, a village in Judah between Jerusalem and Gaza.

Many feel that the third view is correct because Nahum was most probably a prophet of Judah, since the Northern Kingdom no longer existed.

D. HIS MINISTRY

1.   THE TIME OF HIS MINISTRY—Seventh Century

It is difficult to determine with precision the exact time of Nahum's ministry. No time element is to be found in the superscription (1:1). However, there is an interesting time reference in 3:8-10 which helps to locate his ministry in a general way.

> "Art thou better than populous *No (Thebes)*, that was situated among the rivers, that had the waters round about it, whose rampart was the sea, and her wall was from the sea? Ethiopia and Egypt were her strength, and it was infinite; Put and Lubin were thy helpers. YET, WAS SHE CARRIED AWAY, SHE WENT INTO CAPTIVITY; . . ."

The city of Thebes *was destroyed* by the Assyrians in 661 BC, the city of Nineveh *will be destroyed* in 612. Nahum had to minister sometime between 661 and 612 because he speaks of Thebes as having been destroyed and predicts that Nineveh will be.

2.   THE BACKGROUND FOR HIS MINISTRY

What was happening between 661 and 612 when the prophet Nahum preached? The Assyrian Empire reached its peak as a world power in the reign of Ashurbanipal (669–633) and steadily declined. Civil strife and rebellion broke out after Ashurbanipal's death (633). At this time Judah is still a vassal to Assyria. In 612 BC, the Neo-Babylonian Empire, with the help of the Medes destroyed Nineveh, and the Assyrians retreated westward to Haran. Thus, Babylon became the imperial master of the Middle East.

II. NAHUM, THE BOOK

THE THEME OF THE BOOK OF NAHUM

One reading of this book makes it clear that the overriding theme is the prophesied destruction of the city of Nineveh and accordingly of Assyria. What happened to Nineveh has happened to many na-

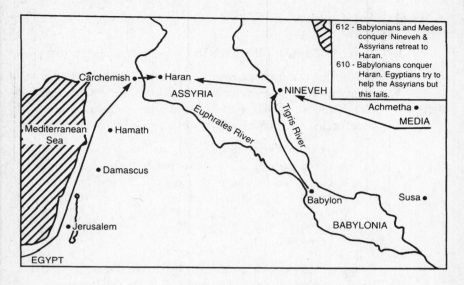

612 - Babylonians and Medes conquer Nineveh & Assyrians retreat to Haran.
610 - Babylonians conquer Haran. Egyptians try to help the Assyrians but this fails.

tions since then in the history of the world. The nation that fears God and honors His word can expect His blessing, but the nations that forget God, though God is mightily longsuffering, will be turned into Hell! The destruction of Nineveh was no stroke of fate. It was the decree of God: *"BEHOLD, I AM AGAINST YOU, DECLARES THE LORD OF HOSTS"* (1:13). How utterly awful to have God be against us! Praise God for the comfort which comes from the Apostle Paul: "IF GOD IS *FOR US,* WHO IS AGAINST US?" (Rom. 8:31b)!

OUTLINE OF THE BOOK OF NAHUM

As with all our studies in the Minor Prophets, the outline of Nahum is based on the theme of the book, which is the Destruction of the City of Nineveh.

I.   THE DESTRUCTION OF NINEVEH DECREED 1

A. THE SERVANT WHO DECLARES THE DECREED DESTRUCTION 1:1

Nahum is given the decree by way of a vision. Remember that a vision is the presenting of the truth of God in pictorial form, whether to the mind or eye. We do not look for visions in this day of grace.

B. THE SOVEREIGN GOD WHO ISSUES THE DECREED DESTRUCTION 1:2-6

This prophesied destruction does not come from the mind of man. Man (Nahum) is only the communicator of the mind of God. He pictures God as "jealous," "avenging," "wrathful," "slow to anger," and "great in power." God will not tolerate a rival to the devotion which he rightly claims from all His creatures. He will pour out His wrath against wicked Nineveh. He is not like puny man, who may plan but may not have the ability to carry out, for He is *GREAT IN POWER*. Therefore, "who can stand before His indignation? Who can endure the burning of His anger?" (1:6). The answer is NO ONE! When the judgment against Nineveh comes, their man-made fortress in which they trust (Zephaniah 2:15) will yield to the Babylonians and Medes, leaving them exposed to the sword and pillage.

C. THE SECURITY OF THE BELIEVER FROM THE DECREED DESTRUCTION 1:7

Nahum tells us that "THE LORD IS GOOD, A STRONGHOLD IN THE DAY OF TROUBLE; AND HE KNOWS THOSE WHO TAKE REFUGE IN HIM" (NASV). Human fortresses will fail. Man-made refuges cannot withstand the might of God. The only safe refuge from the storms of judgment is GOD, HIMSELF! As Martin Luther put it long ago: "A MIGHTY FORTRESS IS OUR GOD, A BULWARK *NEVER FAILING!*" Paul tells us in Colossians that our "life is hid with Christ in God!" An ancient fortress was the last safe refuge in battle, and even it could fall. Security for the believer in the day of judgment is found only in God.

D. THE SEVERITY OF THE DECREED DESTRUCTION PICTURED 1:8-12a

Having presented the truth that the LORD has intimate care and concern for those who trust Him, Nahum now presents the contrasting truth. The language he uses to picture the severity of the decreed destruction is awesome: (1) "Overflowing flood" (v. 8); (2) "a complete end" (v. 8-9); (3) "consumed . . . stubble completely withered" (v. 10); (4) "cut off and pass away" (v. 12).

History is mute testimony to this destruction. Let us be sobered by the fact that there is a far greater and more awesome judgment awaiting all those who will not make Christ their refuge (Rev. 20:11-15).

E. THE SALVATION WHICH COMES AS A BY-PRODUCT OF THE DECREED DESTRUCTION 1:12b-15

Judah has been experiencing the chastisement of God. Assyria has been the instrument of this chastisement, bringing Judah under their yoke. "Though I (the Lord) have afflicted you (Judah), I will afflict you no longer. So now, I will break his (Assyria's) yoke bar from upon you, And I will tear off your (Judah's) shackles" (1:12b-13 NASV). The destruction of Assyria would be so complete that not only would they be destroyed, but they would become extinct ("your name will no longer be perpetuated" 1:14a NASV). What good news this will be for Judah! Verse 15 pictures a fleet-footed runner arriving in Judah to announce the destruction of Nineveh which spells peace and comfort for Judah. You can just hear the messenger's cries as he comes for Judah. "NINEVEH IS DESTROYED! NINEVEH IS DESTROYED!" What rejoicing and shouting. Now Judah can get back to normal religious life—celebrating their feasts and paying their vows.

The Apostle Paul speaks of another fleet-footed messenger in the book of Romans (10:15). That messenger is the herald of the good news of the gospel which brings peace to the sinner when he believes. Praise God for all those who have taken this message of good news far and wide in this sinful world! Have we taken it to our neighbors and friends?

II. THE DESTRUCTION OF NINEVEH DESCRIBED 2

Remember that Nahum is actually seeing this destruction happen—in a vision. Thus he *VISUALIZES* it in dramatic form—just as it happens. We enter into the battle with him, but, like himself, we are just by-standers. We see the invader come, we hear the noise of battle, we see the confusion in the city, we watch as people flee and as the invaders (Medes and Babylonians) take over.

A. PRELUDE TO THE SEIGE 2:1a

The enemy approaches Nineveh: "The ONE (Babylonians and Medes) WHO scatters has come up against you" (NASV).

B. PREPARATION AGAINST THE SEIGE 2:1b

The Assyrians are pictured as getting ready against this
invasion: "Man the fortress, watch the road; strengthen your
back, summon all your strength" (NASV). Of course, it will
be of no avail!

C. PROMISE RELATED TO THE SEIGE 2:2

Assyria's downfall will be Judah's liberation (see 1:12-15). "For
the Lord will restore the splendor of Jacob . . . even though the
devastators (Assyria) have devastated them (Judah) . . . ?
(NASV).

D. PICTURE OF THE ARMY OF THE SEIGE 2:3

The invading army of the Babylonians and Medes is seen decked
out in exquisite battle array—shields . . . battle dress . . . chariots
. . . spears.

E. PRESSING OF THE SEIGE 2:4-12

Nahum is looking right in on the seige (vision). He graphically
describes it: Chariots are raging in the streets (v. 4), the army is
fighting for the wall (v. 5), the gates of the river are opened (v. 6),
captives are taken (v. 7), people are fleeing (v. 8), the city is sacked
(vv. 9-10a), tremendous fear prevails (v. 10b), the leaders are
defeated (under the figure of lions), (vv. 11-12).

F. POSTSCRIPT TO THE SEIGE 2:13

The postscript tells us that the reason Nineveh fell was God's
doing: "I AM AGAINST YOU, DECLARES THE LORD OF
HOSTS" (2:13a NASV). A summary is given of the extent of the
destruction:

1. Destroyed *Military*—"burn up her chariots."

2. Destroyed *Governmentally*—"a sword will devour your
    young lions."

3. Destroyed *Economically*—"cut off thy prey"

4.   Destroyed *Diplomatically*—"no longer will the voice of your messengers (ambassadors) be heard."

The ambassadors demanding tribute and submission will be silenced.

This summary of destruction has been repeated over and over in the history of the nations as they have arisen, only to fall. The most memorable in modern history is Nazi Germany.

III. THE DESTRUCTION OF NINEVEH DESERVED 3:1-7

God is not acting arbitrarily with Nineveh; He never does with any nation or individual. Nineveh's destruction comes because they deserve it. God judges on the basis of His holiness. When men and nations violate His holiness, He must, and will, intervene.

A. NINEVEH'S SINS IDENTIFIED 3:1-4

Nineveh's sins were violence, falsehood and plunder (3:1); ruthlessness and cruelty (3:2-3); seduction and subjection of the nations (3:4). Some want to understand verses 2, 3 as referring to the invasion of Nineveh in chapter 2. It is better to take them as a description of how Nineveh invaded other citadels and left corpses in its wake. These sins have been repeated over and over again by other nations through the centuries and they will continue to be committed until our Lord returns to earth to set up His kingdom.

B. NINEVEH'S SINS PUNISHED 3:5-7

1.   Description of It (3:5-6)

In the Old Testament days there was the practice of exposing to public view and shame a woman convicted of unchastity (see Hosea 2:3). Even so, Nineveh, which has seduced the nations, will become a spectacle to the nations when God exposes her to His judgment.

2.   Effects of It (3:7)

Nahum tells us that when Nineveh falls, *NO ONE WILL MOURN*. They have been a menace in the earth. They have raped the nations. They have brought violence and cruelty to mankind. GOOD RIDDANCE!

IV. THE DESTRUCTION OF NINEVEH IS DEFINITE 3:8-19

What God decrees (chapter 1), what Nahum describes (chapter 2) and what Nineveh deserves (3:1-7), is DEFINITE (3:8-19)—it is assured of happening in spite of Nineveh's attitude and misplaced trust. Nothing can thwart the decree of God!

A. NINEVEH WILL SHARE THE FATE OF NO-AMON (Thebes) 3:8-13

Nahum says to Nineveh: "are you better than No-Amon (Thebes) . . . ?" No-Amon was better fortified and situated than Nineveh, and they had allies on their side—YET THEY FELL! No-Amon was destroyed in 661 BC and the Assyrians were the victorious invaders. Nineveh is NOT BETTER THAN NO-AMON! They too will fall. Nahum says: "YOU TOO WILL BECOME DRUNK, YOU WILL BE HIDDEN. YOU TOO WILL SEARCH FOR A REFUGE FROM THE ENEMY" (v. 11). This either means that Nineveh will be overthrown in the midst of a drunken orgy, or they will drink the full cup of God's wrath. There is no doubt that they drank the cup of God's wrath. According to Diodorus, the Assyrian king and nobles were attacked by the enemy while they were in the midst of a drunken orgy. When the attack takes place, both Nineveh's *FORTIFICATIONS* (described as fig trees with first ripe figs which can be gathered with a minimum of exertion) and the *PEOPLE* (described as women) will fall with ease. The Bible says that PRIDE COMES BEFORE A FALL. Nineveh was proud, boastful, and arrogant, as seen in Zephaniah 2:15: "This is the exultant city which dwells securely, who says in her heart, *I AM, AND THERE IS NO ONE BESIDE ME.* How she has become a desolation, a resting place for beasts! Every one who passes by her will hiss and wave his hand in contempt." How utterly awful is ARROGANCE! In the New Testament, proud, boastful Peter learned his lesson, and he passes it on to us: "Humble yourselves . . . under the mighty hand of God, that He may exalt you at the proper time . . ." (1 Pet. 5:6 NASV). The way up is the way down. The man who loses his life is the man who gains it.

B. NINEVEH'S EFFORTS AT DEFENSE WILL BE
FUTILE 3:14-19

Nineveh will not be able to do anything to save themselves! The challenges which Nahum throws out are all exhortations given in irony. Go ahead, prepare for the battle. Store up water (v. 14), strengthen your fortress (v. 14), multiply your soldiers (v. 15)! But no effort will succeed (vv. 15a, 17-18)! NO, NINEVEH'S WOUND IS INCURABLE! (v. 19), and when it dies there will be universal joy. "All who hear about you will clap their hands over you, for on whom has not your evil passed continually?" The destruction of this wicked nation is an historical illustration that the nation that forgets God will be turned into hell. It points to that day when all the nations of the earth will be gathered before His glorious throne and "He will separate them from one another, as the shepherd separates the sheep from the goats; and He will put the sheep on His right hand, and the goats on the left . . . Then He will also say to those on his left, Depart from Me, accursed ones, into the eternal fire which has been prepared for the devil and his angels; . . ." (Matt. 25:32-33, 41). When that day of judgment is complete, then the nations of the earth which have acknowledged Jesus Christ as Savior will go into the Kingdom of God on earth to reign with Christ for 1,000 years (Matt. 25:34). Let us look with hope to the future when our Lord will put down all rule and all authority by His coming and will then reign supreme in righteousness and holiness.

CHAPTER

8

The Book
of Zephaniah

Do you know how to cry? Do you know what it is like to have great sorrow in your heart? Have you had the experience of seeing something very precious to you fall apart and disintegrate? If you can answer yes, then you can enter in, somewhat, to the feelings of Zephaniah as he watched his precious nation Judah and Jerusalem, corrupt itself morally, religiously, and spiritually and thus fall apart as a nation. Zephaniah wanted to do something about it. He wanted to be used by God to stem the flood-tide of iniquity that was drowning the nation's very life. So, like Jeremiah and Habakkuk, he lashed out against people and leaders with an awesome message of coming judgment, describing his people as a nation that *"KNOWTH NO SHAME."* He cried out that "the day of the Lord is near"—that day when God in fiery judgment would pour out his wrath on sinners. He painted a dark, dark picture, but, as bad as it was, he held out hope if Judah would repent (2:1-3). We know they did not heed the message, for 2 Kings 25 records their national destruction at the hand of the Babylonians. However, like several of the other minor prophets, Zephaniah speaks of the future day (3:9-20) when Israel would be converted and restored as a nation. Zephaniah's description of that future time is one of the most beautiful in the Old Testament. It is touching and tender and full of joy. God has not finished with His ancient people, and this last passage gives light in the darkness, hope amidst sin and sorrow, the promise of salvation after destruction.

I. THE MAN, ZEPHANIAH

A. HIS NAME

Zephaniah means "Jehovah shall *hide,* or *conceal*." There are four men in the Old Testament with this name. A play on the prophet's name occurs in 2:3: "PERHAPS YOU WILL BE *HIDDEN IN THE DAY OF THE LORD'S ANGER*" (NASV). The Lord is pictured many times in the Bible as a place of refuge and safety for His people. Paul says in Colossians 3:3 regarding New Testament believers, "YOUR LIFE IS *HIDDEN* WITH CHRIST IN GOD" (NASV). The poet has phrased it: "O SAFE AND HAPPY SHELTER, O REFUGE TRIED AND SWEET."

B. HIS PERSONAL HISTORY

We know next to nothing about the personal history of Zephaniah. However, it is interesting to observe the ancestry of this servant of God given in 1:1: "ZEPHANIAH, the son of Cushi, son of Gedaliah, son of Amariah, SON OF HEZEKIAH . . ." (NASV). If the Hezekiah (KJV = Hizkiah) mentioned here is the King of Judah who bore that name (2 Kings 18-20), then Zephaniah's ancestry is traced back to royalty—in other words, he was a member of the royal house. He is the only Old Testament prophet of whom this is stated. It is interesting to note that being a member of the royal house did not cause him to compromise his prophetic ministry, which included sharp condemnation of the princes and king's children (see 1:8, 3:3).

C. THE MINISTRY OF ZEPHANIAH

1. THE TIME OF HIS MINISTRY
(1:1; compare 2 Kings 22-23; see your chart)

"The Word of the LORD which came to Zephaniah . . . *IN THE DAYS OF JOSIAH,* son of Amon, king of Judah:" King Josiah reigned from 640 BC–609 BC. He was just a small boy (8 years old) when he began his reign, so it is obvious that others handled the affairs of the kingdom for him until he himself was capable.

Josiah was a very spiritual man. Whoever cared for him as he was growing up had a good influence on his life and character. 2 Chronicles 34 shows Josiah's spiritual progress. At the age of 16 he began to seek the Lord (2 Chronicles 34:3). Four years later, Josiah began to cleanse the land of all the tokens and instruments of idolatry (2 Chronicles 34:3-7). At the age of 26, he started repairs on the temple in Jerusalem. It was during this time (2 Kings 22:8-13) that the Book of the Law (Genesis through Deuteronomy) was found. Evidently Manasseh, the wicked king of Judah who ruled for some fifty years, had so obliterated the worship of Jehovah through his idolatrous measures that even the Scriptures were destroyed. But a copy was found, evidently among the rubbish heaps in the temple. When Josiah learned its contents and the judgments which God had promised for gross idolatry, he humbled himself (2 Kings 22:11), sought counsel of the Lord through Huldah, the prophetess (22:13-20), then forced a revival which was the most far-reaching the nation had ever seen (23:1-20).

This revival was followed by the celebration of the Passover (23:21-23). The writer of 2 Kings says concerning Josiah: "LIKE UNTO HIM WAS THERE NO KING BEFORE HIM, THAT TURNED TO THE LORD WITH ALL HIS HEART, AND WITH ALL HIS SOUL, AND WITH ALL HIS MIGHT, ACCORDING TO THE LAW OF MOSES" (23:25). Unfortunately, the revival was only in Josiah's heart and not in that of the nation. Thus, all the measures he took in destroying idolatory had no lasting effect upon the hearts of the people. How much Zephaniah's ministry contributed to the revival we do not know. Zephaniah is not mentioned in the record of the Kings. It is not surprising that, when Habakkuk ministers just a few years later (609–597), after the death of good King Josiah, the nation has returned to idolatry.

2. **THE INTERNATIONAL SITUATION AT THE TIME OF HIS MINISTRY**

The Assyrians were getting closer to the end of their power over the nations. In 626, Nabopollassar, an Assyrian general who was in charge of Babylon, rebelled against the empire and became founder of the Neo-Babylonian Empire of which Nebuchadnezzar, his son, later became king. The Neo-Babylonian Empire, along with the Medes, invaded Nineveh and destroyed it in 612 BC. Zephaniah had prophesied the destruction of Nineveh (Zephaniah 2:13-15). When Zephaniah prophesied the coming destruction of Judah and Jerusalem (1:4-2:3 & 3:1-7), it was to be at the hands of the Babylonians. The Babylonians invaded Judah three times (605, 597, 586) and carried off captives. The last time (586) they destroyed Jerusalem. All the preaching of Zephaniah, Habakkuk, and Jeremiah, plus the reforms of Josiah, could not turn the stiffnecked people of Judah back to God. They had passed the point of repentance, though God's gracious invitation was still extended.

II. THE THEME OF THE BOOK

The theme of Zephaniah is the *Judgment and Blessing of God*. Judgment is the subject of 1-3:8, and Blessing of 3:9-20. The judgment is not only directed toward Judah and Jerusalem, but against several surrounding nations. All of these predictions were fulfilled to the letter. The blessing aspect of Zephaniah's prophecy includes, as well, both Israel and the nations. This part of the prophecy is yet-to-be-fulfilled. In developing the theme, Zephaniah uses the term "day of the Lord" and its synonyms— "that day," "day of wrath," "at that time"—several times. We should be reminded that this term speaks primarily of God's intervention into the affairs of men in judgment.

OUTLINE OF THE BOOK

I. THE JUDGMENT OF GOD 1-3:8

A. JUDGMENT UPON THE WHOLE EARTH 1:1-3

This judgment which is to affect the whole *earth* (NASV) is pictured generally in 1:2 and then specifically in 1:3. Scholars differ in their time-selection of this universal judgment, but many place it in the yet-future when Jesus comes. The language is awesome and terrible and would seem to fit the judgment of God during the Tribulation Period (Revelation 6-19). The church will not be on earth at that time.

B. JUDGMENT UPON JUDAH AND JERUSALEM 1:4-2:3

1.   WHOM WILL THE JUDGMENT AFFECT? 1:4-13

Zephaniah has a long list: The wicked idolaters (vv. 4-6); the unrighteous royal house (vv. 7-8a); the godless aristocracy who ape foreign ways (v. 8b); violent men (v. 9); worldly merchants (vv. 10-11); and the cowardly indifferent (v. 12). He gives us a picture of a totally corrupt people—of a nation destroying itself through its own corruption. When something is corrupt, it is good for nothing but to be thrown on to the garbage heap. So will it be with Judah and Jerusalem; so will it be with any individual or nation that forgets God. But when will this happen?

2.   WHEN WILL THE JUDGMENT COME? 1:14

"Near is the great day of the LORD, Near and coming quickly . . ." How this should have spoken to Judah and Jerusalem! As corrupt as they were, there was still opportunity to repent, but we know that they did not. Theirs was not a problem of procrastination-of putting off something until it was too late. They just could not conjure up the moral determination, even in the face of imminent destruction. God's people should learn from this! How awful is the condition of a man who is so corrupt that he does not have the moral ability to repent!

3.   WHAT WILL THE JUDGMENT BE LIKE? ... 1:15-17

The description is awesome and geared to strike terror into the hearts of sinners. The distress of the Day of the Lord will cause absolute disorientation ("walk like blind men" NASV) and will lead to death. Why? "Because they have sinned against the Lord" (NASV). Sometimes the harsh message of judgment is needed, but those who are stiff-necked and dull of hearing will not respond.

4.   HOW CAN ONE ESCAPE THE JUDGMENT TO COME? 1:18-2:3

a.   *Negatively*— 1:18

Zephaniah makes it crystal clear that material wealth—that which can bribe a judge to make a favorable decision—cannot bribe God. "Neither their *silver* nor their *gold* will be able to deliver them on the day of the LORD's wrath." God "plays no favorites." His arm cannot be twisted. But is it possible to escape the coming wrath?

b.   *Positively*— 2:1-3

The answer is *REPENTANCE!* This nation "without shame" must turn from sin before the "burning anger of the Lord" comes upon it. Even the meek and humble (and there were some) must seek the Lord, righteousness and humility (v. 3). God's servants have always proclaimed this message. The apostle Paul preached "repentance toward God and faith in our Lord Jesus Christ" (Acts 20:21). Judah and Jerusalem did not heed the message and they reaped the judgment. All who refuse the message of the gospel today will be eternally banished from the presence of God (Revelation 20:11-15).

C. JUDGMENT UPON THE SURROUNDING NATIONS 2:4-15

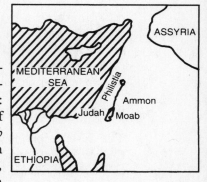

The nations which are denounced for sin and threatened with judgment are: *Philistia* on the West coast of Palestine; *Ammon* and *Moab* just east of the river Jordan and the Dead Sea; *Assyria,* which is the greatest power on earth at the time of Zephaniah but which is rapidly falling apart since the death of Ashurbanipal; and Ethiopia, the most remote enemy of Judah. The nation of Israel has always been surrounded by enemies. Even today, Israel is an insecure nation, surrounded by neighboring nations which feel that Palestine should be theirs.

1.   JUDGMENT UPON PHILISTIA 2:4-7

The Philistines were a strong people that settled along the sea coast of southwest Palestine. Their land was about 50 miles in length and 15 miles wide. They were strong rivals of Israel from the time of Joshua until David's reign. They were idolaters like all the other surrounding nations and at times dominated Israel. Zephaniah prophesied that they would be cut off in judgment (four cities are mentioned) and their land would become Israel's.

2.   JUDGMENT UPON MOAB AND AMMON 2:8-11

Moab and Ammon were descendants of Lot and thus were blood relatives of Israel (Genesis 19:31-38). From Lot's two sons, who were born through incestuous relationship, came two peoples who were always a thorn to Israel. Their arrogance, and their taunting of God's people would cease for God will make them like Sodom and Gomorrah—a perpetual desolation. Then Israel will have their land. Arrogance is always the loser!

3.   JUDGMENT UPON ETHIOPIA 2:12

The Ethiopians in the south were the most remote people known to Judah. They had attacked Judah in the days of King Asa (2 Chronicles 14:9-15). Just as God mightily defeated them then, so His sword of judgment would fall on them once again.

4.   JUDGMENT ON ASSYRIA 2:13-15

Remember that the whole book of Nahum is devoted to predicting the doom of Assyria. Zephaniah portrays the detestable arrogance of Assyria in these words: "This is the exultant city which dwells securely, who says in her heart, *I AM, AND THERE IS NO ONE BESIDE ME!*" We know that Nineveh was so smashed to pieces and buried that no one knew for centuries if it had even really existed until it was rediscovered in the middle of the nineteenth century. Nations that build on arrogance and all the sins which come from that haughty attitude have written their own death warrant! It is the humble and the lowly that God will establish.

D. JUDGMENT UPON THE CITY OF JERUSALEM 3:1-7

Someone has said "A city is first the ambition and then the despair of man . . . Men are proud of a city; they name themselves by its name; they sun themselves in its power and splendor, and yet in the hands of men, the city has become a *MONSTER* WHICH DEVOURS CHILDREN." Jerusalem at this time was a monster because its citizens and leaders were monsters! What an indictment Zephaniah brings against the city! It is a city *WHICH KNOWS NO SHAME!*

1.   The Portrayal of Jerusalem's Sin 3:1-4

Generally, the city is portrayed as "filthy," "polluted," and "oppressing" (KJV). Specifically, its *citizens* are seen as rebellious—unwilling to hear the voice of the Lord through the prophets, unwilling to receive instruction and trust in the Lord (3:2). And what of its leaders? Politically and judicially, they are wild animals in their treatment of the people; religiously, they pollute God's house and do violence to the law by callously violating it (vv. 3-4). Are there not cities like that today? Do we pray for cities like this? Are we faithful messengers of the life-changing gospel to the cities? Can a city be reached? Was Nineveh (Jonah 3)? Could Jerusalem be changed? The opportunity for change was still open (2:1-3). What did they do with it? The next section tells us.

2.   The Persistence of Jerusalem's Sin 3:5-7

a.   God's PRESENCE did not deter Jerusalem from its pursuit of sin 3:5

"The Lord is *righteous* within her; He will do no injustice. Every morning He brings His *justice* to light; He does *not fail. BUT THE UNJUST KNOWS NO SHAME.*"

The Lord—the righteous, holy faithful Lord—was in their midst. "Every morning" through the ministry of the prophets He brought "His justice to light." But did this cause them to repent? NO! They were so debauched that it could be said of them that they knew no shame. Conscience had ceased to function, and the distinction between right and wrong was so blurred and dulled. Can this happen today to a believer? Absolutely. We must judge ourselves and keep short accounts with God.

**b.   God's POWER manifest in judging other
       nations did not deter Jerusalem from its
       pursuit of sin** 3:6-7

In His righteous anger God severely judged unrighteous nations. They deserved what they received from His powerful hand. These nations had far less light than Judah and Jerusalem. The more light one has, the more responsible one is (v. 6), but Israel did not get the message. The Lord said, "I said, Surely you will revere me, Accept instruction" (v. 7), but they did not. HOW SAD! Many men and women since then have followed the same route. In the face of God's great love and tender mercy they have gone their own way. There is no darker sin than to despise the mercy of God. Rejecting Him is doing just that.

E. JUDGMENT UPON THE WHOLE EARTH 3:8

Zephaniah now does what so many of the prophets do. They leave a situation where judgment is somewhat imminent and local, and leap over the centuries to a time of judgment which is future and universal. This verse refers to the Battle of Armageddon, referred to in Joel 3:9-16 and Revelation 9:11-21. It is at this time that Jesus will come and put down all earthly rule and authority. Yes, it is going to happen some day. God will see to it that it does, and we who know the Lord will accompany Him back to earth in His victory train. What an honor!

II. THE BLESSING OF GOD 3:9-20

The book of Zephaniah does not end in judgment. Like so many of the minor prophets, he speaks of great blessing ahead for God's true people. These few verses survey some of this blessing for both Gentiles and Jews.

A. THE FUTURE CONVERTED NATIONS OF THE WORLD 3:9-10

The previous section ended with the judgment of the nations—those who reject Christ during the tribulation period (Revelation 6-19). But many Gentiles will be cleansed of sin in that day and become pure worshipers of God. Purified lips that call on the Lord are the result of purified hearts. "Blessed are the pure in heart" (Matthew 5). One of the evidences of salvation is the content of one's speech. Many have testified that before they were saved their speech was vile and repulsive, but after conversion they began to use their tongues to "sing our great Redeemer's praise."

B. THE FUTURE CONVERTED NATION OF ISRAEL 3:11-20

1. The CHARACTER of Converted Israel 3:11-13

In the past, Israel was characterized by shame, arrogance, unrighteousness, and fear of their enemies. "In that day," that is, the future day of the Lord when Jesus shall put down all rule and all authority at His coming to earth, Israel will not only be converted *BUT CHANGED!* Shame will be removed and will be replaced by the confidence of God's forgiving love (v. 11a). The arrogant rebels will be changed into a humble and lowly people who will trust, *NOT* in themselves (or in works, or idolatrous images, or foreign alliances), *BUT IN THE LORD*—the Lord whom they rejected and crucified, and of whom they said, "we will not have this man to reign over us" (vv. 11b-12). Unrighteous living will be replaced by holy living, and because of this Israel will have no fear. Fear is a great motivator to sin. It causes people to lie, cheat and trust in things which cannot help (v. 13). A holy people is a trusting people, and a trusting people has no cause for fear.

Are the *fruits of change* being manifested in our lives? Jesus said, "you shall know them by their fruits." "If any man be in Christ, he is a new creature . . ."

2. **The JOY of Converted Israel** 3:14-20

A truly converted people will be a joyful people. Joy in the heart must come to the surface. Here the Lord commands that Israel express their joy with exuberance—"Sing . . . shout . . . be glad . . . rejoice *WITH ALL THE HEART* . . ." But what has Israel to rejoice over? The answer is given in one of the most beautiful passages in the Old Testament. Basic to all of God's blessings is *God's presence.* Israel is assured that *"the LORD IS IN THE MIDST" of them.* What does this mean for Israel? It means that their judgment is over (v. 15a), their enemies have been cleared away (v. 15b), their fear is removed (vv. 15c-16), their LORD exults over them, and is quiet in His love for them (v. 17), their shame will be turned into praise (vv. 18-19), and they shall be a "renown and praise among all the peoples of the earth, . . ." God has promised all these things unconditionally for His people, AND THEY WILL SOME DAY BE A REALITY FOR THE CONVERTED NATION! God does not lie, and He is faithful to His promises! Not all the promises in the Bible are for the church, but can we not rejoice as we read this passage and thank God for His great goodness and grace to His ancient people? Can we not rejoice that we experience right now many of the things mentioned in this passage as promised to Israel? Is not the Lord with us (Hebrews 13:5). Has not the Lord conquered our enemy, Satan, at the cross (Hebrews 2:14-15)? Does not the Lord exult over His bride, the church (Ephesians 5:25-27)? Is there any reason why the believer in Christ should be overwhelmed by fear (Revelation 1:17)? Yes, the believer in this church age has reason to "Sing . . . shout . . . be glad . . . (and) rejoice with all the heart."

9

The Book of Habakkuk

BEWILDERMENT! PERPLEXITY! OUTRAGE! "God, where are you? Don't you care about what's going on down here on earth? How can you be so indifferent in the face of all this wickedness and iniquity? Why don't you do something about it?" Have you ever felt this way? Have you ever thrown these questions into the face of God? Maybe you haven't, but the Prophet Habakkuk did! How outraged he was at what was going on in his own nation! Certainly if he were so terribly bothered by it, then God, the HOLY GOD, would be more so and should do something about it. Why, it is unthinkable that the HOLY GOD would be indifferent to such depravity! Throughout the centuries people have asked the same questions with the same spirit of outrage concerning the problem of the continued presence of evil in our world. Some have asked these questions from a skeptical and agnostic point of view. They have not been men of faith. Habakkuk was not a skeptic. He was not a doubter! He had a tremendously strong faith in God. Habakkuk believed that God knew what was going on in Judah, but he couldn't understand why God had not, thus far, done anything about it. Though a man of faith, and a holy man of faith at that, he was impatient. He is like a lot of us who think that we know better than God, and that God should jump at our every cry. Well, God had been doing something all along about the awful depravity of Judah (1:5 NASV), and He had His own timetable. Habakkuk must learn to wait on the Lord and be of good courage. Though He could not see the hand of God at work, he must believe that God was actively involved in doing something about the problem of which Habakkuk complained. We can learn a lot from Habakkuk. His dialogue with God in the first two chapters is extremely instructive for our faith in God.

I. THE MAN, HABAKKUK

A. HIS NAME

Habakkuk's name means to "embrace" or "to cling." In a spiritual sense, this is exactly what he did in relation to God. The meaning of his name suggests his perseverance in holding fast to God in faith, in spite of the puzzling questions which filled his mind. What a lesson for us! When we face problems, we need to cling to God in faith. We must not let the "mystery" of a situation overwhelm us to the point of doubt and despair. We must always remember that an *all-wise* and *all-loving* God is on the throne. He always does what is right.

B. HIS PERSONAL HISTORY

We know nothing for certain about this. The rabbis speculated that he was the son of the Shunamite woman in the time of Elisha the prophet in the 9th century BC This speculation was based on the meaning of his name, "EMBRACE." Elisha said to the Shunamite woman, "At this season next year you shall *EMBRACE A SON*" (2 Kings 4:16 NASV). Once again, it must be said that our inability to trace a prophet's background does not in any way hinder us from understanding and appreciating his prophecy. After all, it is the Holy Spirit—the Spirit of prophecy—who gave us this book. The prophet was only His mouthpiece.

C. THE MINISTRY OF HABAKKUK

1. THE TIME OF HIS MINISTRY

a. *Generally,* it was during the time when the Neo-Babylonian Empire was in power. Though Habakkuk does not mention a king in the superscription of his book, he does mention the rise of the Chaldeans (Neo-Babylonian Empire) in 1:5-6. The Neo-Babylonian Empire started in 626 BC when Nabopolassar, the father of Nebuchadnezzar, rebelled against the Assyrians and took over Babylon. Later, along with the Medes, he defeated the Assyrians (612 BC). The picture portraying the Chaldeans in 1:6-11 is evidence that they were already making their way through the middle-east making conquest after conquest. Judah would be next.

b. *Specifically,* Habakkuk prophesied *after* the fall of the Assyrians in 612, *but before* the first invasion of Judah by the Babylonians in 605 BC Can we narrow it down even further? Yes. The moral and social wickedness which Habakkuk describes in 1:1-4 fits well the reign of Jehoiakim who ruled in Judah from 609 (after the death of good King Josiah) to 597. Josiah had forced a reformation in Judah (622–609), but after his death the nation reverted to their old ways under King Jehoiakim. The prophet Jeremiah gives a scathing indictment of Jehoiakim for his wicked ways and acts (Jeremiah 22:13-23).

2. THE PLACE OF HIS MINISTRY

Habakkuk, of course, was a prophet of Judah. His prophecy does not say that he lived in the city of Jerusalem, but it can be safely inferred that he was in residence there. His mention of the moral and social evils best fits Jerusalem (1:1-4). The fact that the prayer psalm (3:1-19) was for the "choir director" (3:19 NASV) implies that he lived in Jerusalem. The choir director was in charge of the Levitical choir and orchestra in that city. Whether Habakkuk knew Jeremiah and Zephaniah who also lived in Jerusalem at this time, we do not know. Certainly he must have heard of Jeremiah.

II. THE BOOK OF HABAKKUK

A. THE THEME OF THE BOOK

The theme is clearly *THE PERPLEXING PROBLEMS AND PRAYER PLEA OF A MAN OF FAITH.* The *PROBLEMS* ARE TWOFOLD (vv. 1-2): WHY is God permitting evil to continue in Judah without doing anything about it (1:1-11); and, once Habakkuk finds out that God is doing something about it, WHY is He handling the situation in the way He has revealed to Habakkuk (1:12-2:20)? Both of these problems are adequately answered for the man of faith. Skeptics and doubters might laugh at God's answers to Habakkuk, but the man of faith is satisfied with God's solutions. The *PRAYER PLEA* (3) comes out of the dialogue of chapters 1 and 2. It is one of the most marvellous psalms in the Old Testament. Habakkuk prays on behalf of his people (3:1-2); sees an awesome vision of the victorious Lord coming to judge (3:3-15); and finally expresses his faith and confidence in the midst of fear and trembling (3:16-19).

B. THE QUOTATION OF THE BOOK IN THE NEW TESTAMENT

Two passages are quoted in the New Testament. Habakkuk 1:5 is quoted by the Apostle Paul in Acts 13:41. Paul seems to use the quote from Habakkuk in an illustrative way for the purpose of warning. Bruce captures the idea: "Great as was the disaster that overtook those (Judah) who ignored the warnings of the prophets, an even greater disaster will fall upon those who refuse the gospel." In Habakkuk's day the disaster that was to overtake Judah was the invasion of the Neo-Babylonian empire. When Paul preached, the disaster was eternal punishment. The second passage (2:4) which will be taken up in the section on the Outline of the Book, is quoted three times in the New Testament.

OUTLINE OF THE BOOK OF HABAKKUK

I. THE PERPLEXING PROBLEMS OF A MAN OF FAITH 1-2

A. FIRST PROBLEM—Why hasn't God done something about the awful moral depravity of Judah? 1:1-4

"Lord, awful depravity is being seen here in Judah and I have prayed and prayed asking you to intervene and do something about it (1:1, 2a). I know you are aware of what's going on, for you know all things, but WHY DON'T YOU DO SOMETHING ABOUT IT? AREN'T YOU CONCERNED ENOUGH TO SAVE YOUR RIGHTEOUS PEOPLE FROM THE SOCIAL INJUSTICES THEY BEAR (1:2b)? Every new day is hard to bear. Every day of the week you cause me to behold awful iniquity and wickedness on the part of the people (1:3a). It is absolutely terrible. Constantly there is violence, destruction, strife, and contention (1:3b). This is plain, indisputable evidence that your law is ignored by sinners and by those who are responsible for enforcing it. There may be a show of justice in the courts but it's only a sham, for justice is never upheld and thus comes out perverted. A case in point is how the righteous in the nation are surrounded by the wicked and cruelly treated" (1:4).

Thus Habakkuk complains to God. He sees the breakdown of morality and law-enforcement. The moral fiber of the nation is so weak that the reforms of Josiah in 622 BC produced no lasting effect. The presence of law is no guarantee of morality. And so it is today. Believers observe exactly what Habakkuk saw. But how do we respond? Habakkuk did the right thing. He prayed about this distressing situation, even though his prayer was somewhat of an indictment against God. Habakkuk's prayer *reveals the holiness* of this servant of God. He was sensitive to the sin in his nation. Habakkuk could not get used to sin, and neither could the small righteous remnant of that time. The prayer also *reveals his confidence*.

He believed that God knew of the awful depravity and could do something about it, otherwise he would not have prayed. But the prayer *reveals his bewilderment*. If God is as sensitive to sin as Habakkuk, why hasn't He done something about it?

What lessons there are for us here! Are we sensitive to sin, or have we become so accustomed to it that it doesn't bother us? Israel was a nation that knew no shame. Are we so burdened about the sin that surrounds us that we ask God to do something about it? Habakkuk may have had his own ideas as to *what God should do* by way of judgment (compare Deut. 28), but one thing is clear: God is not indifferent to sin and He is at work to bring about changes. We can be assured that God, in His own time, will intervene.

B. GOD'S ANSWER TO THIS PROBLEM 1:5-11

God is sovereign. He has a plan and a timetable to execute His plan. He reveals that to Habakkuk now. He says, "I will intervene, and it will be in your day" (1:5). I am going to chastise Judah for their sin and I will use the Chaldeans (Neo-Babylonian Empire) as my instrument of judgment (1:6). The Neo-Babylonian Empire crushed the Assyrians in 612 by destroying Nineveh. So the nation that desolated the greatest empire on earth would be used of God to chastise Judah. A description of their power, cruelty, brutality and violence is given (1:7-11), and Judah will be easy prey. "Yes, Habakkuk, I have been working on this problem all the time, and I am doing something about it." What a lesson for us to learn. We might ask in our impatience, "Where is God? Why doesn't He do something about it?" But God is always working. He may not do things as we think He should, nor accomplish them at the time we would hope, but God is still on the throne. He is still in control. We can trust His wisdom, AND HIS SEEMING SILENCE! When God answers our perplexity, it may stagger us and cause more bewilderment. That's just what happened to Habakkuk.

C. SECOND PROBLEM—How can God use such a wicked instrument to judge Judah? 1:12-17

"God's response to the first problem brought no final satisfaction to Habakkuk. Instead of lifting the prophet's burden, God added to it. The answer to the previous puzzle left Habakkuk with a thornier one. He just could not see how God could justify the use of wicked instruments to scourge the more righteous inhabitants of Judah" (D. Hubbard).

Habakkuk expresses hope, based on the character of God, that when the judgment comes, it will not annihilate God's covenant people ("We will not die."). He faces the fact that God has "appointed them to judge . . . establish them to correct" (1:12), but he thinks that God is acting contrary to His *holiness* (using wicked Babylon as His chanstising instrument—1:13). He also sees an apparent contradiction of God's mercy (1:14-17). Using very vivid imagery, Habakkuk portrays Babylon as a fisherman sitting beside a well-stocked stream of humanity and drawing in catch after catch. When the fisherman has eaten to his satisfaction, he goes back to fishing again. Judah is a part of the fish in the stream. The fishing equipment represents the armies of Babylon and their weapons, which the Babylonians worship by attributing their success to their might (1:14-16). Will the merciful God allow the continued merciless slaughter of His people? Will there not be an end to it? Habakkuk is simply appalled. How will God answer?

D. GOD'S ANSWER TO THIS PROBLEM 2:1-20

Though overwhelmed, Habakkuk was not hopeless. The desperation which he felt in 1:14-17 will now be relieved. However, God's answer is not an explanation of the *seeming* contradiction between His acts and His character—that is, God as a holy and merciful God doesn't seem to be acting that way. God does not always answer our perplexities in the way that we think He should. Many questions are left unanswered and faith responds, SO BE IT. But a threefold answer is given:

1.   THE FIRST ANSWER 2:1-4

Habakkuk prepares for God's answer by *WAITING*. In 1:1-4 he was impatient, but he has learned that he must "wait on the Lord." His willingness to wait implies that he is a man of faith (2:1). The prophet knew that His great God would not disappoint him. He expected His God to answer and knew that he must wait on Him. The answer came in vision form (2:2a); it was to be published for public knowledge (2:2b); it will take place in God's own good time (2:3a); and it is certain of fulfillment (2:3b). But what is the answer? It is one which only men of faith can understand: "BEHOLD, AS FOR THE PROUD ONE, HIS SOUL IS NOT RIGHT WITHIN HIM; *BUT THE RIGHTEOUS WILL LIVE BY FAITH*" (2:4 NASV). Habakkuk had expressed the hope (1:12), *"We will not die."* God now confirms this by declaring that the righteous remnant in the nation at the time of Habakkuk "will live." The prophet has "laid down the principle by which faith, that is humble, steadfast reliance upon God's word, was declared to be the instrument to bring about the well-being and security of the covenant people (righteous in the nation at the time)" (D.W. Kerr).

Habakkuk 2:4 is quoted three times in the New Testament (Romans 1:17; Galatians 3:11; Hebrews 10:38,39). The New Testament does not quote this verse as though it is a *FULFILLMENT OF A PREDICTION*. Rather, it is used as the *CONFIRMATION OF A PRINCIPLE*. Faith is the principle. Let us demonstrate this by comparing Paul's use of it in Romans 1:17 with Habakkuk's.

HABAKKUK—A word for an ominous situation:

a. *WHO?*—Israel the nation.

b. *PROBLEM*—Sin of the nation (apostasy).

c. *THREAT OF JUDGMENT*—The Babylonian scourge and captivity.

d. *RESPONSE*—Habakkuk prays.

e. *DESIRE*—The physical survival of the righteous remnant.

f. *PROMISE*—Shall live physically. They will not die when the Babylonians invade.

PAUL—A word for an ungodly world:

a. *WHO?*—Both Jews and Gentiles.

b. *PROBLEM*—Sin of the whole world.

c. *THREAT OF JUDGMENT*—The Damnation of God (wrath).

d. *RESPONSE*—Paul preaches.

e. *DESIRE*—Justification of all who believe.

f. *PROMISE*—Shall live eternally, having been justified on the principle of faith.

Faith was the key to survival in Habakkuk's day, and faith is the only condition for living eternally with God.

Believers should be reminded that we live our lives in the same way that we were saved and justified—by faith! Paul, the great New Testament man of faith, said: "WE WALK BY FAITH, NOT BY SIGHT" (2 Corinthians 5:7). Faith is always based on *facts*, otherwise it is pure fancy. The facts are the very words of God in the Bible. To live by faith, then, is to daily take God's word to heart—consenting to, believing, and obeying it. The more we KNOW of God's Word, the more we can walk by faith. Ignorance of God's Word is a great hinderance to the life of faith. Do we study it regularly (2 Timothy 2:15)?

2.   **THE SECOND ANSWER**—The Babylonians' doom is assured 2:5-19

"As the righteous remnant will be preserved, so the haughty oppressor will be destroyed. This fate is announced in the form of a taunting proverb pronounced by the nations which the Babylonians have victimized" (J. Graybill).

Five woes are pronounced against the Babylonians:

a. *The Woe Given Against Aggression.* The accumulation of other people's property was achieved by lustful force. Babylon will reap what it has sown. It has sown violence, it will reap violence (2:5-8).

b. *The Woe Given Against Evil Gain.* This gain they desire for the purpose of self-fortification. They really sin against themselves for this is what others will eventually do to them (2:9-11).

c. *The Woe Given Against Tyranny and Inhumanity.* Not only did the Babylonians build their palace with the spoils of war, but they used slave-labor in constructing and strengthening cities. Habakkuk reminds God's people that God's will is not finally fulfilled in earthly empires but in the spreading of the knowledge of His glory through the earth. The empire builders of the world are doomed to failure, in spite of any apparent success, because God's final program has room for only one universal sovereign—THE CHRIST! (2:12-14).

d. *The Woe Given Against the Humiliation of Captive Nations.* The Babylonians made their subject-nations involve themselves in vile practices. The law of sowing and reaping will be applied to them. The Persians will some day humiliate the Babylonians. (2:15-17).

e. *The Woe Given Against Idolatry.* Any nation whose trust and confidence is not in the Lord cannot succeed. Idolatry is so stupid. By worshipping idols, men actually humiliate themselves, for they give honor and respect to something which they have made with their own hands, and thus something far inferior. An idol is helpless to support a person in a time of need, and since it is speechless it cannot give any counsel. The New Testament warns: "Little children, keep yourselves from idols" (1 John 5:21). Don't give your worship to anything or any one except God. (2:18-19).

3.   **THE THIRD ANSWER**—The sovereign
Lord is ruling 2:20

*"BUT THE LORD IS IN HIS HOLY TEMPLE. LET ALL
THE EARTH BE SILENT BEFORE HIM" (NASV)*. What
great implications we find in this verse. First, Habakkuk and
God's righteous remnant need not fear or fret, for God is on
the throne. He is in control of the situation. Second, He can
be trusted no matter how perplexing the situation seems.

Someone has said, "There is a ring of finality in this verse.
The furious clamor of the Babylonians, the growing panic of
Judah, the passionate questioning of the prophet—all these
must yield in silence to the sovereign will of God. The
righteous judge of all the earth will do right."

II. THE PRAYER PSALM OF HABAKKUK, THE MAN OF FAITH 3

Habakkuk, this great man of faith, has voiced his bewilderment to
God. God has answered him, and Habakkuk has accepted God's
answers even though they have not been exactly as he thought they
should be Habakkuk has been hushed into silence as far as any further
complaint is concerned. Now he will open his mouth in prayer, not
to complain, but to petition.

A. THE PRESCRIPT TO HIS PRAYER 3:1

This chapter, though different in form from chapters 1 and 2, is
nevertheless the work of Habakkuk. God inspired him to give
this prayer. The word *SHIGIONOTH* is of uncertain meaning.

B. THE PETITION OF HIS PRAYER 3:2

"LORD, I HAVE HEARD THE REPORT ABOUT THEE AND
I FEAR. O LORD, REVIVE THY WORK IN THE MIDST OF
THE YEARS, IN THE MIDST OF THE YEARS MAKE IT
KNOWN; IN WRATH REMEMBER MERCY." This is the only
plea in the prayer psalm. Habakkuk has heard the report of the
coming judgment (1:1-17) and he is afraid. He prays that God
would show mercy in the process of bringing judgment. We know
He did this because a remnant was spared from death and later
came back to Palestine after the Babylonian captivity.

C. THE PICTURE RECEIVED IN VISION—FORM DURING HIS PRAYER 3:3-19

1. The Vision Given 3:3-15

The vision is that of a *past event*. Usually in Scripture a vision portrays events to come, but this vision is a *POST-VIEW* of the mighty, victorious Lord as He brings His people through the wilderness toward the promised land. He is pictured as going before His people in awesome power, startling and astonishing and defeating the nations while bringing salvation to His own people. Nothing can stand in the way of this might Conqueror! He is invincible! BUT WHY SHOULD GOD GIVE HABAKKUK A VISION OF SOMETHING WHICH HAPPENED CENTURIES BEFORE? The reason seems to be this: Just as God was invincible in leading His people to victory and judging the nations in the process, so now, because of Judah's sin, He will be invincible in leading Babylon against Judah and Jerusalem; nothing can halt His march to accomplish His will. This vision has an awesome, but wholesome, effect on Habakkuk.

2. The Vision Responded to 3:16-19

The thought of God's fearsome judgment brought terror to Habakkuk's heart, but there is nothing he can do about it. It is God's will, so he will simply accept it and wait quietly for the invasion of the Babylonians (v. 16). *Terror* and *resignation* are not the only responses. Though devastation and deprivation will come, Habakkuk will exult in the Lord—the Lord who will be his salvation and that of the righteous remnant. *Exultation* turns into *exhilaration*, for Habakkuk is imbued with a fresh vitality which could only be compared with the swiftness of a deer. What a lesson for us! Even in the dark and awesome days the believer can joy and exult in God. God will be our salvation. Let us praise Him!

10

The Book of Haggai

Repent! Get right with God! Put first things first! Then God will be glorified and you will be blessed! That's the story of Haggai. But from what are they to repent? And what is to be at the top of their priority list? In Habakkuk we left God's people *on the verge of the Babylonian captivity.* But in Haggai, *the captivity in Babylon is over* and the people are back in their land—Judah.

These restored people have become wayward again. O MY! Not more idolatry, social injustice, and immorality? No, nothing like that. The nation has been purged from idolatry through their chastisement in Babylon, and the other evils have not yet reappeared. Then what is the problem? It is the same problem that we have in the church of God today—a problem which has left the church in a weak and powerless state worldwide. IT IS THE PROBLEM OF MATERIALISM—putting things and money in the place of the Lord and His will for our lives.

The New Testament says: "Seek ye first the Kingdom of God and His righteousness and all these things (the basic necessities of life) will be added unto you" (Matthew 6:33). But we are not satisfied with just having food and clothing and a place to live. We have to "make it big in this world," and in our desire to possess more and more, Biblical priorities go out of the window. Thus, the church for which Christ gave Himself (Ephesians 5:25) suffers weakness and defeat, and the Lord is dishonored. If Christ loved the church and *gave Himself up for her,* should we not love the church too, and give ourselves up for her?

Israel had come back from captivity and had made an attempt to put "first things first." They started to build God's top priority project— THE TEMPLE. In faith they built the ALTAR and LAID THE FOUNDATION (Ezra 3), but when certain circumstances arose in which they did not exercise faith (Ezra 4), fear dominated them and they stopped building. From *faith* to *fear* to *materialism!* When you turn your eyes from the Lord, you get defeated. When you are defeated, you don't live for God—you live for yourself. Thus, Haggai is sent to a people whose mind is set on material possessions—on houses and lands, while the house of God and the work of God suffer. "You cannot serve God and mammon!" (Matthew 6:24).

When Haggai rebukes the people for their materialism, he does not tell them that it is wrong to have nice things—even *a lot* of nice things. He rebukes them for their preoccupation with materialism to the extent that it has displaced the Lord and His will. God will not tolerate this in His children. For the sixteen years that they have ceased from their building activities He has been chastising them right where it hurts most—the economy and the pocket-book! You cannot rob God and get away with it! Haggai calls the people to consider their ways—to get right with God so that His will might be accomplished, that He might be glorified, and that His blessing might be experienced.

I. HAGGAI, THE MAN

A. HIS NAME

The name *HAGGAI* means "festal" or "festive". The first three letters of his name, *HAG*, is the Hebrew word for "feast" in the Old Testament. Some think that this prophet was named HAGGAI because he was born on one of the great feast days of Israel. Others hold that his name simply refers to *joy*. It is interesting that, when Haggai gives his second sermon (2:1), it is preached on the last day of the feast of Tabernacles. Tabernacles was the most joyous feast of the Jews. Certainly, the completion of the rebuilding of the temple was a time of great festive joy for the restored people of God.

B. HIS PERSONAL HISTORY

Theories abound concerning Haggai's background. One tradition holds that he was carried into the Babylonian captivity as a very small boy and returned to Judah when Cyrus gave the decree allowing the Jews to go back to their land to rebuild the temple. If this were true, he would be a very old man when he prophesied, because the captivity to Babylon was for 70 years (Jeremiah 25:12;

29:10). This is a theory, but it is entirely possible, because we know from Ezra 1-6 and Haggai that some who returned to Palestine had been living in Judah or Jerusalem before the Babylonian captivity took place (Haggai 2:3; Ezra 3:12).

C. HIS MINISTRY

1. THE TIME OF IT

Haggai's prophetic ministry is extremely easy to date. Both his prophecy and Ezra 1-6 give us adequate dating. In the first verse of his book we read: "In the *SECOND YEAR OF DARIUS* the king, in the *SIXTH MONTH,* in the *FIRST DAY OF THE MONTH,* came the word of the LORD by Haggai the prophet . . ." The king mentioned is Darius the First (Hystaspes) who reigned over the Persian Empire from 521 BC to 486 BC. This Darius is not to be confused with *Darius the Mede* who ruled the city of Babylon as a sub-king under the great Cyrus. Haggai's ministry started in 520 BC (see your chart) which was the second year of Darius I's reign. (Ezra 4:24-5:1). Before the captivity the ministry of the prophets was dated by Jewish kings, but now by Gentile kings because Judah is dominated by foreign powers and there are no more Jewish kings. The "times of the Gentiles" (Luke 21:24) is in full swing.

2. THE BACKGROUND OF HIS MINISTRY—Ezra 1-6

Heathen Rulers	Dates	Jewish Leaders	Number	Project upon Return
Cyrus the Great	539 BC	Zerubbabel Joshua	Approx 50,000	The rebuild-rebuilding of the Jewish temple which had been
Darius I	520 BC	Haggai Zechariah		destroyed by Babylonians.

The historical background for Haggai's ministry is found in the first six chapters of Ezra. These chapters tell of the *first return* of Jews from the seventy-year Babylonian captivity. Cyrus the Great, the first ruler of the new Persian Empire, issued a decree to allow the Jews to return to their homeland. Approximately 50,000 Jews responded and followed the leadership of Zerubbabel back to the province of Judah. Their primary mission was to rebuild the temple (Ezra 1). In about 536 the temple project began with erection of the altar and laying the foundation of the temple (Ezra 3). Not long after this the temple work was stalled by interference from neighboring peoples (Ezra 4) and stopped completely. Fear over-whelmed the Jews as they took their eyes from the Lord. Fear is the culprit which causes a lot of good work for the Lord to cease!

For a period of some 16 years nothing was done to complete the project, and the Jews found the existing situation an excuse to become heavily involved in their own affairs. The Lord sent Haggai and Zechariah to rebuke the people for their materialism and disobedience, and to stir them up to PUT FIRST THINGS FIRST (Ezra 5:1,2; Haggai 1:1-15). The Jews were challenged again (Ezra 5:3-6:13): this time they kept their eyes on the Lord and finished the work (Ezra 6:14-22). They had learned their lesson—that *fear brings defeat* and opens the door for many other sins, but the *faith accomplishes the will of God* in spite of the odds and brings untold blessing. "Faith, mighty faith that promises, and looks to God alone, laughs at impossibilities, and says, "IT SHALL BE DONE!" Is that the kind of faith we have?

3. **THE COMPANION-PROPHET OF HIS MINISTRY**—Zechariah

Zechariah prophesied along with Haggai in stirring up the people. He was just a young man at this time (Zechariah 2:4) but had some very encouraging things to say to the people. He proclaimed that the Holy Spirit would be their strength, that all obstacles would be removed, and that Zerubbabel would indeed finish building the temple (Zechariah 4:6-9). If Haggai was an old man at this time, then their relationship was something like the Paul-Timothy relationship of the New Testament. It is a grand thing for a young preacher to have the fellowship of a veteran worker. On the other hand, it is a stimulating experience for an older worker to have the fellowship of a young, enthusiastic preacher. May there never be a generation gap in spiritual things (1 Peter 5:5).

II. HAGGAI, THE BOOK

A. THE THEME OF THE BOOK

The theme of Haggai is very simple and practical. It is *THE RE-BUILDING OF THE JEWISH TEMPLE* by the returned captives from Babylon. Remember that this is the theme of Ezra 1-6 as well. Regarding this theme, Haggai gives four messages: The *first message* is given to *rebuke the carnal citizens* of Judah and Jerusalem and *to stimulate them to get back to their first duty* in rebuilding the temple (1:1-15). The second message *encourages the newly revived people* and leaders to *CONTINUE* rebuilding, for they have become discouraged after a month of re-construction (2:1-9).

The *third message assures the people* of the return of God's favor in their agricultural efforts since they have become obedient in rebuilding the temple (2:11-19). *The fourth message* is intended to encourage the leader of the rebuilding program, Zerubbabel. He is instructed that God will put down all nations and kingdoms— inferring the liberation of the Jewish nation from foreign domination—that that he, Zerubbabel, will be a type of the Messiah who shall some day reign (2:20-22).

There are many, many practical lessons for the modern Christian to be found in these four sermons. Christians are involved in the building of the Body of Christ, the Church. How are we getting on with this? Is it a top priority in our lives? Have we grown discouraged in the process so that we want to give up? Have we discerned God's favor in our lives by way of spiritual blessing for having committed ourselves, our lives, to building the church? Are we imbued with the hope that the gates of Hell shall not prevail against Christ's church, and that it will ultimately overcome the world? These and many other parallels can be seen in the book of Haggai. Let us be encouraged by its *principles* and its *parallels*.

B. THE FOUR MESSAGES OF THE BOOK OF HAGGAI

The four messages are primarily exhortative in nature. They are geared to stir up, to motivate to action. The predictions of future events (2:6-9; 2:20-22) are given for the purpose of encouragement. These four messages were preached over a period of four months and are all well-dated (see the chart below). Zechariah, a companion prophet of Haggai, preached some of his messages during the same period. You can observe where his first two messages fit in with Haggai's ministry. The year of this ministry is the second year of Darius I (520 BC).

First	Second	Third	Fourth
6th Month last day	7th Month 21st day	9th Month 24th day	9th Month 24th day
1:1-15	2:1-9	2:10-19	2:20-22

Zechariah 1:1-6 First Message Given in the 8th month.	Zechariah 1:7-6:15 Second Message Given in the 11th month.

OUTLINE OF THE BOOK

This is a sermon geared to *REBUKE* the people for their carnal priority—MATERIALISM—and to *REVIVE* the people to a Biblical priority.

Keep in mind that the altar and foundation of the temple have been standing for 16 years. Now they are saying: ". . . THE *TIME* HAS NOT COME, EVEN THE TIME FOR THE HOUSE OF THE LORD TO BE REBUILT"

(NASV). Good Bible teachers have not been unanimous as to the meaning of the expression, "THE *TIME* IS NOT COME." Two views have been offered:

a. *First,* that the word "TIME" refers to the *PROPHETIC* time for building God's house. Note the logic in this view: (1) We started work on the temple with good intention; (2) we have been greatly hindered by the enemy and have been forced to stop; (3) if it were really the right *PROPHETIC TIME* to build the temple, then we would not be having all this trouble. This view presupposes that the 70-year Babylonian captivity was to be figured from 586 BC and find its completion in 516 BC. The people's excuse is that they have misinterpreted God's timing and that the 70-year Babylonian captivity is not to be figured from 605 BC—when the Babylonians first subjected Judah and Jerusalem and took captives off to Babylon—but from 586 BC when the city of Jerusalem was destroyed by the Babylonians and the third deportation of captives took place.

b. *Second,* the word "TIME" refers to the *adverse circumstances* in which the returned captives are living—surrounded by unfriendly neighbors, difficult economic problems, etc. The argument goes something like this: (1) We are a struggling little community with too many problems to handle; (2) we must get these out of the way first; (3) then we can think about finishing the temple.

The second view is more appealing, for if the people had had the first view, then Haggai and Zechariah would have given them instruction on the *dating of the Babylonian* captivity. Rather, Haggai's answer is: "IS IT TIME FOR YOU YOURSELVES TO DWELL IN YOUR PANELED HOUSES WHILE THIS HOUSE LIES DESOLATE?" (1:4).

Carnal religious people are always looking for excuses to "do their own thing." The excuse of the Jewish people in Haggai's day has been one used over and over again by professing Christians. It is the "ME FIRST" attitude that is behind all selfish interests.

2.   **THE RE-EVALUATION OF THEIR CARNAL PRIORITY CHALLENGED** 1:3-4

This challenge comes in the form of a question, and the obvious answer to the question is NO! Thus the need to reevaluate their priority. Their houses are of far less importance than the house of God and yet their houses are elegant and God's house lies desolate. What an indictment. What is our priority? Is it God's interest or our own? Remember, Haggai is not rebuking the people for having nice things, but for having them at the expense of God's house.

3.   **THE RESULTS OF THEIR CARNAL PRIORITY.** 1:5-6

How long the Lord let the people prosper during the sixteen-year (536-520 BC) period that the temple lay unfinished, we do not know. Now, however, they are experiencing an economic recession. Instead of living on easy street, they are suffering in their pocket books and economy, learning that you cannot rob God and get away with it!

4.   **THE REPENTANCE FROM THEIR CARNAL PRIORITY EXHORTED** 1:7-8

Haggai calls upon them to "consider their ways!"—to realize their selfish life-style, condemn it and turn away from it. Once they do this they can get on with putting God first in their lives and glorifying HIM. "GO UP TO THE MOUNTAINS, BRING WOOD AND REBUILD THE TEMPLE, THAT I MAY BE PLEASED WITH IT AND BE GLORIFIED, SAYS THE LORD" (1:8). Are we taken up with our own things to the extent that the work of God lies desolate and incomplete? If we are, then God calls upon us to CONSIDER OUR WAYS! TO REPENT! Completing the temple would not be easy ("Go up to the mountains, bring wood . . ."), but God would be *PLEASED* and *GLORIFIED*. So it is with building Christ's church. It is not easy work, but it pleases our Head, Jesus Christ, and brings glory and honor to His name! Isn't this what you want most in life?

5. **THE RATIONALE FOR THE FAILURE OF THEIR ECONOMY** 1:9-11

When bad times come our way, we gripe and complain— especially when our basic needs in life are affected. There must have been plenty of complaining by the people as they were frustrated in their agricultural efforts—efforts extremely important to sustain their lives from day to day. Haggai points out that what is happening to them is no "freak of nature." He makes it crystal clear that God has been chastising them. As a loving Father, God is seeking to correct the people through economic pressures. Praise God, it worked! How about us? Are we sensitive to the chastening hand of the Lord? When bad times come to us, do we have the sense to say, "Lord, are you trying to tell me something?"

B. **THE SPIRITUAL PRIORITY OF THE PEOPLE REGAINED** 1:12-15

The challenging message of Haggai brought a positive response from a humbled and contrite people. The challenge of 1:7-8 was heeded, bringing REVIVAL!

1. **THE REVIVAL OF THE PEOPLE OF GOD** 1:12

OBEDIENCE AND REVERENCE! That's the key to true Biblical revival! The people said from their hearts, "We will do the will of God. We will put Him first in our lives." They probably showed their REVERENCE by bringing sacrifices to the altar to atone for their sins. Do you need revival in your life? It begins with OBEDIENCE in renouncing sin and pledging your life to do the will of God.

2. **THE REVIVAL OF THE WORK OF GOD** 1:13-15

God's work cannot be revived without a revived people. A wonderful promise is given to this renewed nation: *"I AM WITH YOU, DECLARES THE LORD"* (1:13 NASV). Haggai does not mean that the Lord had personally left them and had now returned. He has always been personally present, but NOW HE WILL BE PERSONALLY PRESENT WITH THEM *IN BLESSING!* The chastisement has been taken away (see 2:11-19).

Christians complain today that their church is not seeing the blessing of God. Why is that? Could it be that God's blessing is being withheld because of a lack of personal revival? "Revive us again: Fill each heart with Thy love; May each soul be rekindled with fire from above!" So, just 23 days after Haggai's first message the work began again.

II. THE SECOND SERMON—A message to encourage the discouraged 2:1-9

Satan hates the work of God! One of his most potent weapons to hinder it is DISCOURAGEMENT. Discouragement is sin, for it means that we have taken our spiritual sight from the Lord and are no longer trusting in his wisdom, love and power. How weakening is discouragement, and how quickly it spreads. Approximately a month after they have resumed working on the temple, the people are in "the slough of despond." Satan has defeated a revived and victorious people! Is this a familiar story as far as your Christian life is concerned? Discouragement is no less a sin than the materialism of chapter one—for both hindered the work of God. One is just as wicked as the other!

A. THE TIME OF THEIR DISCOURAGEMENT—"21st day of the 7th month" 2:1

What is so significant about this day? It so happens that the 21st day of the 7th month was the last day of the week-long Feast of Tabernacles. Tabernacles was the most popular and joyous feast of the Jews, but there is no joy in Israel now. How pathetic! Discouragement turned their joyous feast into a funeral! Discouragement kills all joy and enthusiasm for the Lord and His work.

B. THE NUMBER OF PEOPLE OVERWHELMED BY DISCOURAGEMENT 2:2

Discouragement has spread to ALL—people and leaders. Not a soul has been left untouched by it except Haggai and Zechariah. The fact that all—people and leaders—are exhorted to "take courage" (v. 4) demonstrates that all have succumbed. But why are they discouraged?

C. THE CAUSE FOR THE DISCOURAGEMENT 2:3

You see, Satan got them to place a value or estimation on their service. Like some Christians, they succumbed to the old game of HISTORICAL COMPARISON. They looked at their endeavor and thought it had very little significance in comparison to "THE OLD DAYS." We all know what it is like when we believe that what we are doing is meaningless. Why, we might as well stop! And that is what they did. But what were they comparing their temple project to? This verse gives the answer: "WHO IS LEFT AMONG YOU WHO SAW THIS TEMPLE IN ITS FORMER GLORY? (Solomon's temple). AND HOW DO YOU SEE IT NOW? (Post-Captivity temple). DOES IT NOT SEEM TO YOU *LIKE NOTHING IN COMPARISON?*" (NASV). Sometimes it is a very dangerous thing to compare. All kinds of sins can emerge: jealousy, discontent, covetousness, etc. But here it was DISCOURAGEMENT. They wanted to give up. Some of them remembered the big, beautiful and costly temple of Solomon, and as they built this tiny, plain, post-captivity structure, they told themselves that God could not possibly be glorified by such a project. It certainly didn't measure up to the "old days." It doesn't always benefit to remember the past. Historical reflection can sometimes be unhealthy as it was here. So the Lord told them the CURE for discouragement.

D. THE CURE FOR THE DISCOURAGEMENT 2:4-9

The cure is twofold: God's *Presence* with them (2:4-5), and God's *Power* to be manifested to them in a future day (2:6-9).

1.   THE PRESENT FACT OF GOD'S PRESENCE ... 2:4-5

Haggai tells them all to *"take courage"* and to *"work."* Why? What will motivate them to obey? The same thing that God promised in 1:13—His Presence! *"For I am with you,* says the Lord of Hosts . . . My Spirit remaineth among you." It is not the vehicle through which God manifests Himself that is important (the temple), but *THE FACT THAT GOD, HIMSELF, IS PRESENT!* Solomon's temple was much bigger and more beautiful than this temple, but God ordered that temple destroyed; thus showing His disapproval of the worship of sinful Judah.

Are you tempted to historical comparison? Be careful; it may be unhealthy and lead to discouragement. Great things have been done in the past, but our responsibility is to do *NOW* what we know to be the will of God. If it is small, don't brand it as unimportant or insignificant. After all, God is with us and working through us. Little is much if God is in it.

2. **THE FUTURE PROSPECT OF GOD'S POWER**.. 2:6-9

Keep in mind that Israel is a small struggling nation, that they are dominated by the great Persian empire, and that they are surrounded by unfriendly neighbors. But God has a grand future ahead for Israel, for He will keep His unconditional promises to them and will reverse the present adverse circumstances. The prospect is that God will intervene in the affairs of earth, bringing judgement upon man's environment (v. 6) and upon nations (v. 7a). Then Jesus will come who is called "the Desire of all nations" (v. 7b), and he will put down all rule and all authority. When this happens, He will establish a new temple more glorious than Solomon's (vv. 7c-9) and the earth will know peace because of His presence.

We are not told what was the effect of this sermon on the people, but we gather from the next sermon (2:10-19) that they must have made a positive response.

III. THE THIRD SERMON—Obedience in building the temple brought the return to God's favor in their agricultural efforts 2:10-19

In chapter one, we learned that God chastised Israel by frustrating them in their agricultural labors (1:5-6; 9-11). Now that they have repented and resumed work on the temple, will God restore His favor upon His people by blessing them in their next growing season? The answer is yes; Haggai *CONFIRMS* the return of God's favor. He begins with an ILLUSTRATION and ends with an APPLICATION.

A. ILLUSTRATION FROM THE JEWISH LAW OF CEREMONIAL CLEANNESS 2:10-13

This is an illustration that the Jews would readily understand and appreciate, though Gentiles may not find it easy to grasp. In the Christian church we do not have anything that parallels *ceremonial holiness*. This was strictly Jewish.

Haggai says, Picture a Levitical priest functioning in the temple and carrying in his long, flowing garments the consecrated flesh of a sacrifice. Suppose that the priest should happen to brush his garment against some other food nearby. Since the flesh he carries is ceremonially consecrated, would this constitute the food that was touched as consecrated as well? The answer, of course, is NO, for the law taught that the garment carrying the flesh would become consecrated but not a third object (Leviticus 6:25-27). Haggai continues his illustration: "Suppose a priest should happen to become *ceremonially unclean* by touching a dead body. Would anything the priest touched become ceremonially unclean too?" Yes, because this is what the law taught.

This is an interesting illustration, but what is the point?

B. APPLICATION OF THE ILLUSTRATION TO THE NATION 2:14-19

Haggai teaches that the nation has been UNCLEAN while living for materialistic pleasures and neglecting their first duty of building the temple. Thus, all the worship that they carried on during that time (536–520) was counted as unacceptable because it was worship carried on by a disobedient people. Now that the people have repented and become obedient, God confirms that "FROM THIS DAY ON I WILL BLESS YOU."

It is tragic to think that all the time Israel was living in disobedience by not building the temple, they were still carrying on their worship at the altar! This reminds us of King David who continued his religious life all during the time of his adultery with Bathsheba and murder of Uriah the Hittite. Finally David, after the searing ministry of Nathan the Prophet, (2 Samuel 12) repented, and he said, "A broken and a contrite heart, O God, Thou wilt not despise" (Psalm 51:17). God despised David's offerings when his heart was full of sin. He despises this type of thing in us too. Many people equate religion with going through certain motions— like church attendance.

This is dangerous, for a man then believes that, if he goes through certain acts of worship, he can live any way he wants—religion covers it all! Religion is only meaningful as it comes from pure and sincere hearts. This is why the Lord said that those who partake of the Lord's Supper should examine themselves. To eat in an unworthy manner at the Lord's Table is to invite chastisement (1 Corinthians 11:27-34).

IV. THE FOURTH SERMON—The leader of the temple building project, *Zerubbabel,* is assured of God's future intervention in victory over the nations 2:20-23

What is predicted in this sermon is definitely connected with the predictions of the second sermon (2:6-9). This is not addressed to all the people, but only to Zerubbabel.

A. ISRAEL'S RELEASE FROM GENTILE DOMINATION 2:20-22

These verses are a capsule prophecy which predict the end of the *"times of the Gentiles"*. They will be fulfilled during the Great Tribulation period and the coming of Christ. What Haggai just briefly predicts, Daniel, Zechariah and other prophets give in detail. This prophecy is directed to Zerubbabel because he is the leader of the nation, the governor of Judah. They would be a great source of comfort and encouragement to him as the leader of the suppressed and down-trodden nation.

B. THE RULE OF CHRIST 2:23

If verses 20-22 tell us of the putting down of Gentile powers, and the rise of God's kingdom in the earth, who then will rule in that kingdom? Verse 23 gives the answer. It will be Zerubbabel! Really? Do we mean that some day Zerubbabel will be resurrected and God will place him on David's throne to rule for 1,000 years?

No! Zerubbabel is a *type* of our Lord Jesus Christ, the One who shall rule. Zerubbabel is used here just as David is used elsewhere as a type of our Lord (see Ezekiel 34:23,24).

Let us take hope in a wicked, restless, and sin-filled world; we know that things are going to change when Jesus comes!

11

The Book
of Zechariah

Can a young person do anything for God—anything of real lasting significance? Well, of course, one can be saved when young and be trained in the Scriptures, but can a young person, even someone in teen-age years, be used of God in ministering to others? In Israel, if a person was of the priestly family of Aaron, he could not begin to *function* as a priest until age 30. That was a long time to wait to commence a public ministry. This was not true of the prophetic ministry, for God set no age limitations on these servants of the Lord. Daniel, Jeremiah, and Zechariah were all young men when they began their prophetic ministry. Who doesn't remember the story of young Daniel and his three Hebrew friends in Babylon? (Dan. 1-6). And who isn't acquainted with the call of Jeremiah when he was but a child (youth)? Then there is the prophet Zechariah whom we are now considering. Zechariah 2:4 reveals that he was just a youth when he received a magnificent vision from God. That vision is recorded in Zechariah 1:7-6:15. Yes, if God wants to, He can use young people to do great exploits in the name of Christ. A young Christian should make himself available like Daniel and Jeremiah and Zechariah to respond to God's direction for Christian service—where and when that should be. God's will is to use people—dedicated people—to accomplish His work on earth. You may never be used to the extent of the great heroes of the Bible, but is it not awesome and wonderful to think that God can use us to accomplish some of His work, no matter what our age or our spiritual gifts! God uses men and women who are useable. One faithful servant of the Lord used to pray, "LORD, USE ME!" Later he realized that he was praying the wrong prayer and the began to pray, "LORD, MAKE ME USEABLE!" His petition changed because his attitude and perspective changed. We will never have to worry about God *using us* in His service if *we are useable,* consecrated believers.

I. THE MAN, ZECHARIAH

A. HIS NAME

The name *Zechariah* is a popular one in the Old Testament, belonging to some 28 different men. It means, "Jehovah remembers." That has great significance for Zechariah's prophecy, for in it he reveals many times over that the Lord has not forgotten *His people,* nor has He forgotten the many *unconditional promises* made to His people centuries before through Moses and the prophets. Zechariah is imbued with the hope of the fulfillment of God's great plan for His people, in spite of the fact that the present circumstances—domination by a foreign power—may seem to contradict God's promises. God does things in His own time. He not only has a plan but He has a timetable for the accomplishing of His plan. Let us *not forget* that Jehovah *remembers!*

B. HIS PERSONAL HISTORY

Very little is known about this. Zechariah came from a priestly family. His grandfather, Iddo, is expressly mentioned as accompanying Zerubbabel, the governor of Judah, and Joshua, the high priest, back to Judah after the Babylonian captivity (Ezra 2:1, 2; Nehemiah 12:1-4). F. B. Meyer speculates that Zechariah's father, Berechiah, "probably died when Zechariah was a small child, and the boy was reared by his grandfather; he is therefore spoken of as the son of Iddo (1:1), and from the earliest his young mind must have been imbued with the traditions and habits of the priestly caste." This is an interesting theory, but it adds nothing to our understanding of the book. Fortunately, a sound interpretation of the book is not dependent upon knowing the details of his ancestry.

C. HIS MINISTRY

1. **THE TIME OF IT**—See Haggai and Ezra 1–6

    This is the same as for Haggai. The dating of his first message is "the eighth month of the second year of Darius" (1:1). Remember that Haggai's first message was given in "the sixth month of the second year of Darius." Generally speaking, the great Persian Empire dominates the Middle East and Judah is subservient to it.

2. **THE NATURE OF HIS MINISTRY**

    It is, first of all, *exhortative in nature*. He preaches to the present needs of the people and challenges them to repent of their sins and to be genuine in their religious and spirtual life. His first (1:1-6) and third (7-8) sermons are in this exhortative category. Secondly, his ministry deals with *predictive prophecies* concerning Israel's future. His second (1:7-6:15) and fourth (9-14) sermons are in this category. It should be noted that these predictive prophecies are meant to be messages of encouragement to the downtrodden nation as they get back to the business of rebuilding the temple and re-establishing themselves in their ancient homeland.

II. THE BOOK OF ZECHARIAH

A. THE THEME OF THE BOOK

The theme of Zechariah is twofold: first, *PRACTICAL MESSAGES* concerning certain aspects of godly living (1:1-6; 7-8). and second, *PREDICTIVE MESSAGES* to inspire faith and hope (1:7-6:15; 9-11). The practical messages concerning godly living were occasioned by certain questions which needed to be answered. The predictive messages were occasioned by the humbled and down-trodden state of the Jewish nation which was struggling for survival and in need of a new prophetic message of hope to rekindle their spirits and embolden their faith. Zechariah beautifully meets the needs of the nation by his prophetic ministry, and his messages come down to us as great words of challenge and powerful words of inspiration and hope.

B. THE REFERENCES TO MESSIAH IN THE BOOK

Like the prophet Isaiah, Zechariah has several references to the coming Messiah, Jesus Christ.

1.   Christ's *entry* into Jerusalem .... 9:9, cf., Matthew 21:5

2.   Christ's *betrayal* by Judas for
     30 pieces of silver .... 11:12–13, cf., Matthew 27:9

3.   Christ being *forsaken* by his disciples in the Garden of
     Gethsemane .... 13:7b, cf., Matthew 26:31b

4.   Christ's *death* .... 13:7a, cf., Matthew 26:31a

5.   Christ's *second coming* to earth to subject all things to
     himself .... 14:3–4, cf., Acts 1:11

6.   Christ being *recognized as Messiah*
     when He comes .... 12:10, cf., Revelation 1:7

7.   Christ's reign as *Priest and King*
     when He comes .... 14:9, cf., Revelation 11:15ff; 19:11

C. THE DATING OF THE FOUR MESSAGES IN THE BOOK

First Message 1:1-6	Second Message 1:7–6:15	Third Message 7–8	Fourth Message 9–14
8th month, 2nd year of Darius I (520 BC)	11th month, 2nd year of Darius I (520 BC)	9th month, 4th year of Darius I (518 BC)	No date given for this message

OUTLINE OF THE BOOK

I. A PRACTICAL MESSAGE CALLING FOR REPENTANCE 1:1:-6

After Zechariah opens his prophecy giving us his *Times* (1:1a), his *Authority* (1:1b), and his *Ancestry* (1:1c), he then launches into his message. Zechariah reminds his hearers that the Lord was very angry with their "fathers" (1:2). These "fathers" were their ancestors who were living in Judah and Jerusalem at the time the Babylonians invaded Palestine and carried the Jews into captivity. They were wicked and unrepentant, so they were punished for their sins. The prophet calls upon the returned exiles to repent of their sins. It is only then that the Lord will remove His hand of chastisement and "return" to them in blessing (1:3).

We can't stand steady dosages of this kind of ministry (nor do we need it on a steady basis), but occasionally someone must remind us of our sins and the need to return to the Lord in repentance. This is the way to God's sure blessing. Notice that Zechariah does not tell them to return to *religion*. They have plenty of that! They need to "get right with God!"

After challenging them to repent, Zechariah warns the returned exiles not to repeat the mistakes of the fathers (1:4-6). The "fathers" didn't listen, or give heed, to the prophets (2 Chronicles 36:15-16). Rather, they mocked them. Thus the fathers reaped God's judgment (2 Corinthians 36:17-21; Zechariah 1:5-6).

Someone has said that "we never learn from history." In a sense, Zechariah is making a plea to the people to *LET HISTORY TEACH THEM!* Why should the children make the same mistakes as the fathers and suffer dire consequences? Should we not pray that we shall be preserved from ignoring the lessons of the past?

II. A PREDICTIVE MESSAGE TO INSPIRE FAITH AND HOPE 1:7-6:15

Zechariah received this message three months after he preached his sermon calling for repentance. Let us note several things in general about it before presenting its outline:

(1) It was received through a vision which Zechariah had during the night.

(2) There are eight distinct parts to the vision; however, the parts are related.

(3) The vision covers a very great span of time, beginning with the period in which Zechariah lived down to the establishing of the (still-future) kingdom of Christ on earth for 1,000 years.

(4) In the vision, Zechariah is accompanied by an interpreting angel who tells him the meaning of many parts of what he sees.

(5) The vision is concluded by the crowning of Joshua the high priest (6:9-15). This crowning is symbolic of our Lord's reign as priest and king in the earth.

(6) The vision was meant to inspire faith in the returned exiles for the day in which they lived, and to inspire hope for the future glory of the nation—a nation now subjected by a foreign power—Persia.

Though the *promises* in the vision are for Israel, not the church, there are abiding *principles* which may be gleaned which the Christian can apply to his life. As you study through these Old Testament prophets, be sure to distinguish between *promises* and *principles*. Nothing in the prophets can be construed as a promise to the church. The church and Israel are two different groups with two different callings, but there are many abiding principles for living which are good for any age.

Now let us see the many parts of the night vision which Zechariah received.

A. THE VISION OF THE HORSEMEN AMONG
THE MYRTLE TREES 1:7-17

1. Vision Presented

In the vision Zechariah sees several things. Note their identity:

a. The *"man riding on a red horse"* is the Lord Jesus Christ (also called in this section "The angel of the Lord").

b.   The riders on the *"red, sorrel and white horses"* consist of an angelic patrol which patrols the earth.

c.   The one whom Zechariah converses with in the vision asking *"what are these?"* is the interpreting angel who reveals the meaning of many parts of the vision in 1:7-6:8.

2.   **Vision Applied**

The meaning of the vision is clear. The divine patrol returns from patrolling the earth. They report to "the angel of the Lord" that the whole earth is "peaceful and quiet." There is no war because the great Persian Empire has subjected the earth, but this is not a happy message for Israel for they are a part of the subjected nations and their temple and city are not rebuilt. A comforting message is then given in the form of a promise. That promise is that God will have compassion on Jerusalem and will return to it in mercy by seeing to it that the temple and city are rebuilt. Other cities of Judah will be rebuilt as well. This promise was fulfilled in Old Testament days: the temple was completed in 516 BC, and the city was rebuilt in 445 BC during the time of Nehemiah.

What an inspiration this vision-message must have been to downtrodden Judah and Jerusalem. It was meant to inspire their faith and increase their hope. So what if Persia dominates the earth. They only do so as God allows! God's promises will be fulfilled. We must always remember that whatever happens in the earth to make us uncomfortable and downcast is *allowed* by God. We must look through these things to Him who sits upon the throne and controls all.

B. THE VISION OF THE FOUR HORNS AND THE FOUR CRAFTSMEN 1:18-21

1.   **Vision Presented**

a.   The *"four horns"* ("horns" are symbolic of powerful nations) refer to four powerful nations which in turn have subjected Judah and Jerusalem—Babylon, Medo-Persia, Greece, and Rome.

b. The *"four craftsmen"* (NASV) are the nations which destroyed the four horns. Thus, Medo-Persia destroyed Babylon, Greece destroyed Medo-Persia, Rome destroyed Greece, and some day Messiah's Kingdom will destroy the Revived Roman Empire which will be headed up by the Anti-Christ (Daniel 2:44-45; Revelation 19:11-21). Messiah's Kingdom, then, is the fourth of the "craftsmen."

2. **The Vision Applied**

The Jewish nation, which is seen as subjected in the first vision, will continue to experience foreign domination until the Lord Jesus returns to earth and puts down all rule and authority (Psalm 2:6-9; Revelation 11:15). The comforting thought to the hearers of this vision is that some day, in God's own timetable, His people will be liberated once and for all by the coming of Jesus. If you are a believer in Jesus Christ, you will return to earth with the Lord Jesus to take part in His victory (Revelation 19:14; 1 Thessalonians 3:13; Jude 14-15). What a glorious honor! Are we living like victors now?

C. THE VISION OF THE MAN WITH THE MEASURING LINE 2:1-13

1. **The Vision Presented**

Let us note the identity of the several characters in the vision:

a. The *"man with the measuring line"* is the Angel of the Lord (Lord Jesus Christ).

b. The *"I"* of verse 2 and the *"young man"* of verse 4 refer to Zechariah.

c. The *"angel who was speaking with me"* is the interpreting angel who accompanies Zechariah in the vision.

d. *"Another angel"* is an angelic being who assists the "Angel of the Lord."

2.   The Vision Applied

This is a wonderful vision of future hope. The "measuring" of Jerusalem is symbolic of the great restoration it will experience in the future millennial age. There will be unparalleled *peace, protection, prosperity,* and *joy*—and all because of the personal presence of Messiah in the earth. What a restoration that will be! Earth has never seen anything like it!

D. THE VISION OF THE CLEANSING OF JOSHUA, THE HIGH PRIEST 3:1-10

1.   The Vision Presented

There are several things to be identified in this segment of the night vision:

a. *"He"* of verse one is the interpreting angel.

b. *"Joshua"* is the High Priest in the time of Zechariah.

c. *"Satan"* is that angelic being who fell into sin and who is presently in rebellion in God's universe.

d. *"Angel of the Lord"* is Jesus Christ.

e. *"Those who were standing before him"* refers to angels.

f. *"Your friends"* refers to Joshua's fellow priests.

g. *"My Servant the Branch"* refers to Jesus Christ.

h. The *"Stone"* also refers to Jesus Christ.

2.   The Vision Applied

Joshua, as high priest, represents the nation of Israel to God. Satan accuses Joshua (and thus the nation) of sin and uncleanness. Satan is rebuked for his accusations and Joshua is then cleansed and attired in clean garments—symbolic of the cleansing of the nation of Israel and their being made fit for priestly service in the earth.

This vision tells us that the future restored Israel will be a spiritually cleansed nation. This cleansing must take place before the restoration can take place. There is a principle here for us. Before fallen, sinful man can be restored to God he must be cleansed by the precious blood of Christ and clothed in His righteousness (2 Corinthian 5:21).

E. THE VISION OF THE GOLDEN LAMPSTAND AND THE TWO OLIVE TREES 4:1-14

1.   The Vision Presented

Once again, let us note the elements of the vision:

a.   A *"lampstand"* all of gold with its bowl on the top of it, and its seven lamps on it with seven spouts belonging to each of the lamps which are on the top of it" (v. 2)

b.   Then, "*two olive trees* by it, one on the right side of the bowl and the other on its left side" (v. 2)

c.   Lastly, "the *two olive branches* which are beside the two golden pipes, which empty the golden oil from themselves" (v. 3)

2.   The Vision Applied

In the tabernacle and temple there was a golden lampstand, but the one Zechariah sees *in vision* (not actual), though having some similarities, is different from it in several respects. In the vision, in contrast to the tabernacle and temple, there are two olive trees and two olive branches on either side of the lampstand which feed oil automatically into the golden bowl at the top and this oil makes its way to the lamps so that they continually burn. In the tabernacle and temple, the priests had to constantly service the lampstand so that its light kept burning.

What does this all mean? The interpreting Angel makes it clear to Zechariah that the vision applies to Zerubbabel, the governor of Judah at the time (4:4-10). Zerubbabel was a godly man who had the responsibility of seeing that the post-captivity temple was built. There had been many problems (external—Ezra 1-6, and internal—Haggai 1) preventing the completion of the temple, but the Jews have been revived in their faith and have begun working on the temple again. Zerubbabel's responsibility to finish the temple could not possibly be done in his own power. God would see to it that the work was maintained and completed by the Holy Spirit (4:6). All the difficulties ("O great mountain") in the way of completing the temple project would be removed ("become a plain"). Zerubbabel laid the foundation and the promise is that he will complete it (temple was completed in 516 BC—Ezra 6:13-22).

Thus, the symbolizing in the vision of the lampstand is *not* in the light that it gives (though that is important), but in the *energy* that produces the light (oil—Holy Spirit). Israel's witness reflected in the rebuilding of the temple would be in the energy of the Holy Spirit.

What a grand principle there is here for us. God's work cannot prosper in man's energy. If we are going to be the light in this dark world that God wants us to be, that light must be produced by the power of the Holy Spirit working through dedicated, useable servants like Zerubbabel. The hymn writer put it aptly, "The arm of flesh will fail you; you dare not trust your own."

The two olive branches mentioned in verse 12 are interpreted in verse 14 as the "two anointed ones, who are standing by the Lord of the whole earth." To stand by the Lord of the whole earth means that they represent Him in the earth as His leaders. These two anointed ones in Israel are Joshua, the high priest (religious leader) and Zerubbabel, the governor of Judah (civil leader).

F. THE VISION OF THE FLYING SCROLL 5:1-4

1. The Vision Presented

We must keep reminding ourselves that we are studying a vision. Many things appear and happen in visions that are very unearthly.

a.   Zechariah saw a *"flying scroll."*

b.   There is writing on both sides of the scroll ("one side." "other side").

c.   The scroll "enters the house of the thief and the house of the one who swears falsely by my name; it will spend the night within that house and consume it with its timber and stones."

2.   The Vision Applied

The scroll is the law of God (ten commandments). On one side of the scroll are written the commandments having to do with our relationship to God and on the other side those which have to do with our relationship to our fellow man. *Stealing* and *swearing* are two things which the commandments disallowed, the former having to do with our relationship to our fellow man and the latter to our relationship with God. The scroll is viewed as visiting judgment upon those who swear falsely by God's name and those who steal. What is the meaning of this? This vision tells us that in the coming day of Christ's kingdom on earth rebellion against the King's law will not be tolerated. Stubborn violaters will be severely judged.

The message for the Christian is one of principle. It doesn't pay to break God's Word. God has given us His Word so that we might be healthy and strong believers in a corrupt and carnal world. To break it is to reap God's judgment.

G. THE VISION OF THE WOMAN AND THE EPHAH 5:5-11

This vision is a good illustration of strange things happening in a vision!

1.   The Vision Presented

a.   Zechariah sees "the *ephah* going forth." (An ephah is a commercial measure which is just a tiny bit bigger than our bushel.)

b.   He sees a *"woman sitting inside the ephah."* Sometimes the Bible symbolizes that which is not in its proper place *spiritually* or *religiously* as a woman.

c.   The woman is thrown down *"into the middle of the ephah"* and a lead cover is cast over the opening—thus incarcerating the woman.

d.   *"Two women"* described as having *"wings like the wings of a stork"* are seen lifting up the ephah and taking it to "the land of Shinar" where a temple would be built for her.

2.   The Vision Applied

This strange vision tells us that in the coming day the evils which have dominated God's ancient people (Idolatry—the woman, and Commercialism—the ephah) will be removed from the Holy Land. Only the Messiah, Jesus Christ, will be honored and adored. Revelation 17 and 18 are New Testament passages which speak of the destruction of these two systems—both of them called "Babylon."

H. THE VISION OF THE FOUR CHARIOTS AND HORSES 6:1-8

1.   The Vision Presented

a.   He sees *"four chariots"* ("four spirits"—angels, v. 5)

b.   These chariots were *"coming forth from between two mountains"* (Mt. Olivet and Mt. Zion).

c.   The mountains were *"bronze"* (bronze is a symbol of judgment)

d.   Horses of various colors pulled the chariots—"red . . . black . . . white . . . dappled" (the various colored horses represent different aspects of judgments brought on the earth).

2.   The Vision Applied

This vision is concerned with world-wide judgment upon the nations. In the first vision, the nations are at ease and Israel is subjected. This vision reverses the situation of chapter one (vv. 7-17), with God using angelic instrumentality, liberating Israel by subjecting the nations. The last battle will be fought in the vicinity of Jerusalem ("two mountains") where the Anti-Christ and his followers meet their end (Zechariah 14:1ff).

Our God is still on the throne. It is just a matter of time—possibly shorter than we realize—when He shall put down all rule and authority, and Jesus shall reign in the earth.

I. THE CONCLUSION—The Crowning of Joshua the High Priest 6:9-15

This is an appropriate conclusion to the night-vision. It is not a vision, but something which happened in Jerusalem regarding Joshua the high priest. Though not a vision, it is rich in symbolism concerning our Lord Jesus Christ of whom Joshua is a type.

1. The Historical Event 6:9-11

Zechariah is commanded to take silver and gold which had just been brought to Jerusalem by Heldai, Tobijah, and Jedaiah—exiles from Babylon. He is to make an ornate crown and to set that crown on the head of Joshua the high priest. The Jews have no king at this time in their history, and certainly a priest, even a high priest, is not eligible to be a king in Judah. What, then, does all this mean?

2. Application 6:12-15

The act of Zechariah in crowning Joshua was symbolic of the fact that our Lord Jesus Christ, when he rules upon His throne, will rule as a King-Priest. He shall bear the glory and will build the future millennial temple which will be the center of the worship of our Lord in the earth.

Earth has never seen a king like this. No earthly sovereign has ever ruled his people with the tender sympathy of a priest, but our Lord Jesus Christ is a "priest forever after the order of Melchizedek." As king He will rule with a rod of iron, as priest He will rule with divine sympathy and love toward His people. He will lead them with tenderness and have mercy on them when they stray.

III. A PRACTICAL MESSAGE CALLING FOR REALITY AND GENUINENESS IN THE RELIGIOUS AND SPIRITUAL LIFE 7-8

This third message is dated in the 4th year, 9th month, and 4th day of Darius I—in other words, in 518 BC. The work on the temple has been resumed now for 2 years; it is probably more than half done.

Haggai and Zechariah have been successful in their ministries. Now a problem arises which is religious in nature. A delegation from Bethel arrives in Jerusalem with a very interesting inquiry to make of Zechariah concerning fasting. The Jews have been fasting and mourning in national humiliation over their calamities since the time of the captivity. The *"fifth month"* was the most prominent time of fasting because it marked the destruction of Jerusalem by the Babylonian army in 596 BC (2 Kings 25:8-11; Jeremiah 52:12-13). But they fasted in other months too: the fast of the *fourth month* commemorated the breaching of the walls of Jerusalem during the final siege (2 Kings 25:3; Jeremiah 39:2-4); the fast of the *seventh month* marked the anniversary of the murder of Gedaliah, governor of Judah (Jeremiah 41:1-18; 2 Kings 25:22-26); the fast of the *tenth month* memorialized the beginning of the siege of Jerusalem (2 Kings 25:1; Jeremiah 39:1). Now that the captivity is in the past and they are reestablished in the Holy Land, should they continue to fast? (7:1-3).

The answer to the question is given in 7:8-10 and 8:16-17. The original question is never answered by a "yes" or "no." Zechariah's answer indicates that there was deeper problem than the question of fasts. The deeper problem was a lack of dedication to the Lord. True dedication would be seen in proper behavior in relationship to their fellow men. In the process of answering the question of the delegation, Zechariah gives some prophetic predictions concerning the coming of the Lord and the establishment of His Kingdom (8:1-8; 8:18-23).

The attitude of the delegation was, "Do we have to keep on doing this?" This is the same attitude that Christians sometimes have. "Do we have to do this? Do we have to do that? Can't we do this?" This kind of attitude demonstrates a real lack of *heart devotion* to Jesus Christ. The attitude of the bondslave of Jesus Christ is, "*LORD*, what will you have me to do?" Let us not call Jesus, *LORD*, and reserve for ourselves our own will.

IV. A PREDICTIVE MESSAGE TO INSPIRE FAITH AND HOPE 9-14

This section is divided into two prophetic messages (9-11 and 12-14). In it there are some prophecies which were fulfilled in the period between the Old and New Testaments (404 BC–4 BC), some in the time of our Lord while He was on earth, and some which are yet to be fulfilled in the tribulation period and kingdom age.

A. THE FIRST BURDEN—Messages which primarily have to do with predictions already fulfilled 9-11

1. Christ, The Great World Conqueror 9

In this chapter the Messiah is contrasted with Alexander the Great. It was Alexander who fulfilled the prophecy in 9:1-8. Alexander was a great conqueror, but Jesus Christ is the greatest (9:9-10). The last part of the chapter (9:11-17) was fulfilled during the period between the Testaments and has to do with conflict between Judah and two of the major divisions of Alexander's empire (the Ptolemies—Egypt, and the Seleucids—Syria) . . . called, *"your sons, O Greece"* (9:13). The eleventh chapter of Daniel is a detailed prophecy concerning these two divisions (vv. 4-35).

2. Christ, The Hope of His People in the Coming Day 10

In the coming day of distress for Israel during the tribulation period, Christ will be their defender. He is spoken of in this passage as the *CORNERSTONE*, the *TENT PEG,* and the *BATTLE BOW.* These three titles tell us what He will be for His people. As the Cornerstone, He is the *Head* of the nation. As the Tent-Peg, He is the *Support* of the nation. As the Battle Bow, He is the *Protector* of the nation. He is all these things to us as well.

3. Christ, The Rejected Shepherd of the Nation 11

This chapter speaks of the first coming of our Savior, when he was sold for 30 pieces of silver. The chapter is not too difficult to understand if you realize that Zechariah is acting out a dramatic parable before his audience. The prophets sometimes communicated their messages in this way (11:4-14). The last few verses have to do with a still-future event when a false shepherd (Anti-Christ) will appear on the earthly scene in the tribulation period. Many from the nations and apostate Judaism will accept this shepherd.

B. THE SECOND BURDEN—Messages which primarily have to do with predictions yet to be fulfilled 12-14

1.   The Invasion of Judah and Jerusalem 12:1-9

This invasion takes place "in that day." This refers to the last part of the tribulation period when Anti-Christ and his forces advance on Jerusalem. God is with His people *in power* at this time, so Jerusalem will be to the enemies "a cup that causes reeling . . . and a heavy stone for all the peoples" (12:2-3 NASV).

2.   The Conversion of Israel 12:10-13:9

a.   **THE TIME OF IT**—"in that day" 12:11

In other words, during the tribulation period (Revelation 6-19).

b.   **THE NATURE OF IT**—"I will pour upon the house of David, and upon the inhabitants of Jersualem, *THE SPIRIT* of grace and supplications:" 12:10a.

Their conversion will be SPIRITUAL in nature, for it will be brought about by the Holy Spirit.

c.   **THE MANNER OF IT**

(1) **God's Part**—"Spirit of GRACE AND OF SUPPLICATIONS" 12:10

God will move toward Israel, the nation, *in GRACE,* removing the judicial blindness (Romans 11:25ff) so that Israel may move toward Him in faith, *supplicating* Him for salvation ("call upon the name of the Lord").

(2) **Israel's Part**—"and they *shall look upon Me* whom they have pierced, and they shall *mourn for Him*" (12:10b).

When God moves toward Israel in grace, they will move toward Christ *in faith* (look upon Him, or to Him) and *in repentance* (mourn for Him). Three illustrations are given to show the depth and genuineness of Israel's repentance in that future day (10c-14).

(3) **God's Part**—Cleansing and the removal of all Satanic agencies 13:1-6.

The fountain of cleansing has always been opened to Israel, but they were blinded and did not see it. That fountain is Christ. When they respond in faith and repentance in the future day, they will be cleansed in their hearts, and their land will be cleansed of idols, the unclean spirit, and false prophets.

d.   **THE BASIS FOR IT**—"Awake, O sword, against my shepherd, and against the man that is my fellow, saith the Lord . . ." (13:7, see also Matthew 26:31a)

The "sword" is the sword of divine justice. This sword is what sinful man deserves, but God caused it to smite His own Beloved Son! God, in His forbearance, "passed over the sins previously committed." Then, at the cross, Christ paid the full penalty that justice demanded. Thus, the sinner goes free. Praise God! Without the cross there can be no conversion for Israel or anyone!

e.   **THE SUFFERING FOLLOWING IT**—13:8-9

Though Israel will be converted in the future day, this does not imply that they will not suffer hardship and even death. Many will die during the "time of Jacob's trouble" (tribulation period) and some will be preserved. This is true of God's people in every age, but especially in that age when gigantic persecution will rage against those who will not receive the mark of the Beast (Revelation 13).

The apostle Paul reminds us that all who live godly lives in Christ Jesus will suffer persecution.

3. The Second Coming of Christ to Earth 14:1-7

Don't confuse the Rapture (catching up) of the Church with
the Second Advent of Christ to earth. The Church will be
caught up to meet the Lord *in the air* (1 Thesselonians 4:13-
18) *before* the seven year tribulation period begins. The
tribulation period will end in the literal second coming of Jesus
Christ to earth. It is this latter truth that is referred to here.
The Church Period is not prophesied in the Old Testament,
but was revealed by our Lord Jesus Christ (Matthew 16:18)
to Peter and later to others (see the teaching of Paul in
Ephesians). The Rapture is an aspect of Church truth and was
revealed to the apostles and prophets of the New Testament.

These verses (14:1-7) relate that the nations will be gathered
against Jerusalem, and then the Lord Jesus will come to the
Mount of Olives (the place from which He ascended to
Heaven—Acts 1:9-12). His coming will mean the end of all
rule and authority for the nations (Revelation 11:15).

4. The Establishment of the Kingdom 14:8-21

At last the stage is set for the final scene of full kingdom
blessing. There will be the appearance of living waters (14:8).
There will be the Kingship of Jesus Christ over "all the earth"
(14:9). There will be geographic changes which will make
Jerusalem a more prominent city. This is consistent with its
status as capital of the world (14:10-11). Of course, all of the
enemies which came against Jerusalem will have been
destroyed (14:11-15). These verses, *chronologically,* would
immediately follow 14:1-3. Then world-wide worship will take
place in the city of Jerusalem, involving Gentiles as well as
Jews (14:16-19). Finally, the prophet concludes his predictive
messages on the note of Israel's holy character *in that day* as
a priestly nation. In the kingdom age, Israel will be a truly
holy nation. No more will it be a scandal among the nations
(14:20-21).

God has great things in store for the converted remnant of
Israel. He is not done with His people. He has not cast them
away forever. Paul teaches us in Romans 11 that Israel is not
TOTALLY nor FINALLY destroyed. He will keep His

unconditional promises made in Old Testament days. *"BLINDNESS* in part is happened unto Israel *UNTIL the fulness of the Gentiles be come in* (until the church age has run its course). AND SO ALL ISRAEL SHALL BE SAVED: *AS IT IS WRITTEN* . . ." (Romans 11:25-26).

What a glorious day is on ahead! The believer in Jesus Christ will be involved in that day, for the Church will return to earth with Jesus Christ when He comes to subdue the earth and establish His 1,000 year reign. But let us not get God's order of events confused. Perhaps a chart will aid in keeping us oriented:

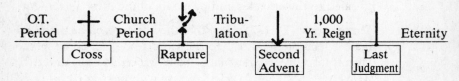

12

The Book of Malachi

So you DOUBT that God really loves you! So you couldn't care less about how you worship God! So you think God's laws concerning marriage are out of date! So you feel that the justice of God is a big joke! So you say, "I'm not going to give any of my resources to the Lord!" So you believe that it doesn't pay to serve the Lord! If this is the way you think and feel, then you have a lot in common with the people of Malachi's day. For all these things, so common today, were true of the people of that time. Doubting God's love for us is probably the most serious of all these, for it sets the stage for a multitude of other sins. If we believe that God doesn't love us, then why should we care about worshipping Him; why should we be concerned about obeying Him by being loyal in our marriages; why should we acknowledge Him as a God of justice; why should we give back to Him a portion of our material wealth; and why should we give our lives in His service?

But God does indeed love us! And when we believe this and realize the implications of it in our personal lives, then we must love Him in return. Our love for Him will be manifest in obedience to His word. Jesus said, "He that hath my commandments, *AND KEEPTH THEM,* he it is that loveth me:" (John 14:21). The nation of Israel in Malachi's day was unevenly divided into two groups: (1) the *great majority* of the nation doubted God's love and were living in outrageous sins; (2) a *remnant* believed God's love (3:16-18) and was characterized by reverence and obedience. What category are you in? Are you a part of the great majority who are living for themselves, or of that small group of believers who could say with the prophet Jeremiah, "Thou hast loved us with an everlasting love?"

I. THE MAN, MALACHI

A. HIS NAME

The name *MALACHI* means "My Messenger." There has always been debate among scholars regarding this name. The debate is this: Are we to understand *MALACHI* to be the *name* of a person, or simply a *title?* Was there a prophet named MALACHI, or was this simply a title designating his prophetic work or office? If the term *MALACHI* was a title, then who bore this title? Those who hold this view say it may have been Ezra. The arguments for this view are too lengthy and involved to repeat here. Suffice it to say that there is no really *STRONG* reason to doubt that this prophet was a person *named* Malachi. What a wonderful name that is. It should remind us that "We've a story to tell to the nations!" Are we faithful ambassadors of the good news of the gosepl to a lost world? Malachi delivered to God's people a message which was filled with rebuke, but it was with the intent of turning them back to God— that they might trust anew in His love for them. That is a worthy goal for all God's messengers. As a communicator of God's word, personally or publicly, what is your motive? What is your goal?

B. HIS PERSONAL HISTORY

There is nothing in the book of Malachi or the historical books of Ezra and Nehemiah which relate his personal history. As in the case of some of the other prophets, it has pleased the Holy Spirit to be silent in this case.

C. HIS MINISTRY

1. THE TIME OF IT

The exact time of Malachi's ministry is not given. However, the following development would seem to put Malachi during the time of Nehemiah.

First, this prophet must have prophesied *after the exile to Babylon* because he mentions a "governor" as being over the land (1:8). This was a political condition which existed when the Jews returned from Babylon. Before the exile, the leader of the nation was a King.

Second, he must have prophesied *after the ministry of Haggai and Zechariah.* Remember that they prophesied during the time of the rebuilding of the temple (520–516 BC). The book of Malachi indicates that the temple has been built and is being used.

Third, certain details link him to *the time of Nehemiah*— especially the later years of his governorship over Judah. Nehemiah came to Jerusalem to be governor in 445 BC. He served for several years in this position and then returned, temporarily, to Persia in 433 BC (Nehemiah 5:14). We don't know how long he stayed away from Judah, but it could not have been very long. When Nehemiah came back, he found gross sin and violation of the law. This is recorded for us in Nehemiah 13. The very "close agreement" between the 13th chapter of Nehemiah and the book of Malachi makes us infer that Malachi prophesied during the return of Nehemiah— within a very few years of 433 BC.

Malachi is the last prophet of the Old Testament. Malachi ends the Old Testament revelation. Following him, there are four hundred years of silence. When that four hundred years is over, the prophet, John the Baptist, appears on the scene to "prepare the way" for the greatest Prophet of all—Jesus Christ.

2.   THE NATURE OF HIS MINISTRY

It is primarily exhortative. There are some future predictions, but Malachi is mainly concerned with ministry designed to rebuke and warn.

II. THE BOOK OF MALACHI

A. THE LITERARY METHOD USED

The reader will observe a recurring method of communication of God's Word. Charges or accusations are made against Israel. These are followed by objections on the part of the accused (in question form). The objections are then answered clearly and without recourse to further argumentation. This method is not used by other prophets, but it is an excellent and effective teaching form.

B. THE THEME OF THE BOOK

The theme of Malachi is crystal clear: *IT IS GOD'S REBUKE OF ISRAEL'S OUTRAGEOUS SINS. THIS THEME IS DEVELOPED IN SIX CHARGES AGAINST THE NATION.* Observe this in the chart below.

I. ISRAEL HAS DOUBTED
GOD'S LOVE 1:1–5

VI. ISRAEL HAS DIS-
CREDITED GOD'S
SERVICE 3:13–4:6

II. ISRAEL HAS DESPISED
GOD'S NAME 1:6–2:9

SIX
CHARGES
AGAINST
ISRAEL

V. ISRAEL HAS DIS-
REGARDED GOD'S
TITHES 3:7–12.

III. ISRAEL HAS DEFIED
GOD'S LAW 2:10–16

IV. ISRAEL HAS DISDAINED
GOD'S JUSTICE 2:17–3:6

OUTLINE OF MALACHI

I.   ISRAEL HAS DOUBTED GOD'S LOVE...................... 1:1-5

Think of all the manifestations in the Old Testament of God's love for His people. Think of the many situations and incidents in which God has demonstrated His love. Is it not incredible, then, that Israel should complain: *"WHEREIN HAST THOU LOVED US?"* (1:2a). We are not told what caused the people of God in Malachi's day to doubt God's love. We are simply faced with the *FACT* of it. The Lord could have given hundreds of examples of His love to assure them, but He answers by referring Israel to their own history—from Jacob down to the time of Malachi: "WAS NOT ESAU JACOB'S BROTHER? SAITH THE LORD: YET I LOVED (preferred) JACOB, AND I HATED (did not prefer) ESAU" (1:2c-5; cp. Genesis 25:19-23). The terms "LOVED" and "HATED" are terms of *preference, not animosity.* God's love for Israel should be obvious! He has always been with the nation—right from the time of Jacob to Malachi's day. God has not forsaken them. How do we know? The very *existence* of Israel *as a nation* is proof. This is in contrast to Esau and Edom. The "HATE" (non-preference) for Esau (Edom) is demonstrated in her destruction as a nation (1:3-5). By Malachi's day, Edom *AS A NATION* dwelling in her rock-fortress was no more. Edom *AS A COMMUNITY OF PEOPLE* moved into Southern Judah (Idumea), but it was no longer a nation. The last we hear of this community is 70 AD when Jerusalem was destroyed by the Romans under Titus.

There is *never* any valid reason to doubt God's love. Life may seem puzzling, but if we just look around, if we investigate long enough, we shall find ample reason to trust rather than doubt His love.

It should be noted that this passage is quoted in the book of Romans (9:13) to illustrate God's sovereign preference in election.

II.   ISRAEL HAS DESPISED GOD'S NAME 1:6-2:9

When we lose our trust in the love of God for us, then everything else in our lives falls apart. That's true in human relationships too—especially in marriage. When you doubt the love of your mate for you, then the whole relationship begins to disintegrate.

Israel has despised God's name. Note how many, many times the word "name" is used in this section. The word "name" does not refer to a proper name or to a title. Rather, it refers to *God's person*—to who He is. God says of Himself, "I AM A GREAT KING" (1:14). What does it mean, then, to despise His name? It means that Israel has dishonored Him. They have not shown the respect and reverence that the GREAT KING deserves. But what proof is there that this is true? The evidence is found in careless worship (1:7-14). The law of Moses taught that only the best animals should be brought as sacrifices to God's altar, but Israel was bringing the sick, the blind and the lame. By bringing such interior offerings they were saying, in effect, "This is what we think of you, God. You are unworthy of our best!" God warned the priests (who are primarily in view) of severe chastisement if they did not rectify the situation. Already, they were suffering (2:1-10).

But we needn't be too severe on Israel of old. All we have to do is take a good look at our own worship! Is it careless, haphazard, ritualistic, half-hearted and selfish? The way we worship tells God what we think of Him. Does He say to us today, "YOU DESPISE MY NAME!" Does He evaluate your worship as lame, diseased, and blemished?

III. ISRAEL HAS DEFIED GOD'S LAW 2:10-16

The Lord turns from rebuking the sins of the priests (1:6-2:9) and severely scolds the defiant people. The people have defied God's law concerning MARRIAGE. It is a case of "like priests, like people"! When the leaders are setting an ungodly example, then the people follow suit.

A. THE HAVE DEFIED THE LAW FORBIDDING MIXED MARRAIGES 2:10-13

The men of Israel had "MARRIED THE DAUGHTER OF A STRANGE GOD" (v. 11). This means that they had intermarried with heathen women who were idolaters. God had expressly prohibited such marriages (Deuteronomy 7:1-5) because they would eventually lead Israel into idolatry (Exodus 34:16).

1. God's Evaluation of this sin 2:10-11

This was a *treacherous act* which in reality was a denial of the *unity* of God as Creator and Father. This act caused *disunity* (especially where divorces of Jewish women were involved) in the nation, and it was a PROFANING OF THE COVENANT GOD MADE WITH THE FATHERS (v. 10b), AN ABOMINATION, AND A PROFANING OF THE *HOLINESS OF GOD (or the sanctuary of the Lord—* NASV) v. 11. God does not speak lightly of it!

2.   God's Punishment of this sin 2:12-13

God will not let His ancient people get away with such acts of treachery. He will severely punish the offenders (v. 12), and no amount of weeping at the altar will cause God to accept the offerings that are brought by the offenders (v. 13).

What a lesson there is here for us. Though times have changed, the principles of God have not. Paul warns in II Corinthians against an "unequal yoke." He commands: "BE YE NOT UNEQUALLY YOKED TOGETHER WITH UNBELIEVERS . . ." (2 Corinthians 6:14). How many, like Israel of old, have ruined their lives, as far as an effective testimony for Jesus Christ is concerned, by marrying unbelievers. This is a treacherous act, and destructive for the believer.

B. THEY HAVE DEFIED THE ORIGINAL INTENTION OF GOD AGAINST DIVORCE 2:14-16

In this section God says, *"I HATE DIVORCE"* (v. 16 NASV). Could that be more plainly said? It was bad enough for the men of Israel to get involved in mixed marriages, but this was made more heinous by the fact that they were *divorcing their Jewish wives* along with it. Jesus said, "What therefore God hath joined together, *LET NOT MAN PUT ASUNDER.*" (Matthew 19:6). The Lord permitted divorce (Deuteronomy 24:1ff) in certain cases "because of the *hardness* of your hearts" (Matthew 19:8), but this was never God's original intention. God's attitude toward divorce is expressly stated in Malachi: *"I HATE DIVORCE!"* We should hate it too! What is divorce?

1.   It is an act of cruelty 2:14

Divorcing one's wife was an act of cruelty because it was not merely the putting away of a woman, but the putting away of a woman who is *"THY COMPANION. . . ."* Here is a woman who has shared her life, and life's experiences, with her husband, and he writes it off as if it were nothing. What cruelty and callousness!

2. **It is an act of disloyalty** 2:14

She is not only his COMPANION, but *"THE WIFE OF THY CONVENANT."* He has vowed his life TO HER. He has left father and mother in order to *CLEAVE* UNTO HIS WIFE! He has vowed NEVER TO LET HER GO! But his vow has turned out to be *empty* words! What disloyalty!

3. **It is an act which frustrates God's design—** "a godly seed" 2:15

This is a hard verse to understand. Perhaps the following paraphrase will help our understanding of it:

> "Did not he (God) make *one* (*one man,* and out of him *one woman,* and the two *one flesh*)? And (yet) the residue of the spirit (of life—Genesis 7:22) was His (so He could, had it pleased Him, created, for example, one man and many women). And why (did He make) the *one*? He sought what only the purity and integrity of the marriage bond can secure—a *GODLY SEED."*

Thus we see, that when a man divorces the wife of his youth and gets involved in a mixed marriage, the issue from that marriage—children—is in jeopardy.

4. **It is an act which FAVORS what God hates—** "I hate divorce" 2:16

The apostle Paul says in Romans 12:9, *"ABHOR WHAT IS EVIL"* (NASV). God hates evil, and we are to have the same attitude toward it. God hates divorce, and His children are to have the same attitude toward it.

In an age and culture which FAVORS what God hates, we would do well to keep a close watch on our marriages, and uphold firmly in our attitude and teaching the Biblical truth—GOD HATES DIVORCE.

IV. ISRAEL HAS DISDAINED GOD'S JUSTICE 2:17-3:6

A. THEIR DISDAIN FOR GOD'S JUSTICE STATED 2:17

The people were saying, "Everyone who does evil is good in the sight of the Lord, and He delights in them, or, Where is the God of justice?" The thought is this: If people are sinning and getting away with it, it must mean that God favors the sinner! What slander! Or, if that is not the case, then God must not exist, because if He did exist, then He would have acted in judgment against the evil doers. Many people through the ages have held the view of the people of Malachi's day. "Why," they say, "if there really were a God, He would not allow war and poverty and evil in His universe!" What this view does not take into account is that (1) God is longsuffering toward sinners and is giving them time to repent and seek forgiveness; and (2) God has a time-table for His judgment. It will come, but it will come in *His* time.

B. THEIR DISDAIN FOR GOD'S JUSTICE RESPONDED TO 3:1-6

It may seem that God is indifferent to the sins of men, but He is not. The Lord is coming, and when He comes He will severely judge. No one will be able to endure the day of His coming, "for He is like a refiner's fire and like fullers' soap. And He will sit as a smelter and purifier of silver, and He will purify the sons of Levi and refine them like gold and silver . . ." The sinners and offenders (v. 5) will reap severe judgment when He comes, but He will not utterly consume His people so as to destroy them forever. This would be a violation of His own character and covenant (v. 6).

There is a contemporary message for us in this ancient prophecy: don't be deluded into thinking that, because God does not immediately judge us for our sins, He doesn't know about them, or is indifferent to them. God is all-knowing . . . nothing escapes Him, and God is never indifferent to sin! It offends Him, and He hates it. His seeming inaction is to be understood as long-suffering toward sinners. The message is: REPENT! Get right with God!

V. ISRAEL HAS DISREGARDED GOD'S TITHES 3:7-12

Tithing was God's way in Old Testament days of providing the means to sustain His work and provide for His ministers, the priests. In Malachi's day, the people were robbing God—they were disobeying clear instruction from His word on what was required (Leviticus 27:30-31; Numbers 18:20-21; Deuteronomy 14:22-23). They were greedy and self-centered in spite of God's goodness to them. How long this had been going on we do not know, but the people were now experiencing God's chastisement and being deprived of His blessing (3:7-9).

What should they do? The answer is simple. They must repent and "bring the whole tithe into the storehouse." If they are willing to do this, God will "open the windows of heaven, and pour out" a blessing on them. He will also remove the chastisement they are experiencing agriculturally (3:10-12).

Many Christians find it difficult to share their material wealth with God's work and ministers. Is it any wonder that some have financial difficulties? A greedy and selfish spirit—especially in the light of all that Jesus has done for us, and the fact that all that we have comes from Him—is a grievous sin! Paul has given us clear instruction in 2 Corinthians 9:6-15 on giving. Are we robbing God, or are we giving cheerfully, proportionately, consistently and regularly to the Lord. "AND GOD IS ABLE TO MAKE ALL GRACE ABOUND TO YOU, THAT ALWAYS HAVING ALL SUFFICIENCY IN EVERYTHING, YOU MAY HAVE AN ABUNDANCE FOR EVERY GOOD DEED;" (2 Corinthians 9:8). If we are not giving to the Lord, let us determine now to do so.

VI. ISRAEL HAS DISCREDITED GOD'S SERVICE ... 3:13-4:6

A. THE MAJORITY IN THE NATION SAID THAT IT DOESN'T PAY TO SERVE THE LORD 3:13-15

These were *arrogant* words against the Lord (NASV). They complained that they were religious—that they had kept His charge, and that they had walked in mourning before the Lord, but it had not been to their profit. God had not rewarded them for it. They complained that God let the "real sinners" get away with their sin and that they were blessed by Him. Of course, this was all a lie. The ones who complained were ungodly sinners. Although they were religious and went through the motions of religious ritual, it was all a sham. It was just superficial and external. They were hypocrites! They had *no heart* for God. Their arrogant complaining was a DISCREDITING OF GOD'S SERVICE.

Have you ever *thought* that "it is vain to serve God; and what profit" is there in it? Unless you straighten out your life by repentance and humility, your "thought" will develop into words of criticism which really are a slander against the Lord. It does pay to serve the Lord if that service comes from hearts that love Jesus Christ and have His glory in view.

B. THE MINORITY IN THE NATION BELIEVED THAT IT DOES PAY TO SERVE THE LORD 3:16-4:3

Among those who *profess* to know God, there is always a remnant who truly are godly. Though the blessing of God may be *delayed* in coming to them, they do not complain that it doesn't pay to serve the Lord. They wait patiently for Him. Three things are said about the godly: (1) they "feared (reverenced) the Lord; (2) they spoke to one another—defending God's actions, and exhorting one another not to lose heart in spite of their hard conditions in life; and (3) they *esteemed* His name—in contrast to the rest in the nation who by their life-style demonstrated that they "despised God's name."

God admires the faith of the humble and meek. This is manifest by His *recognition* of them in Malachi's day: "gave *attention* and *heard* it, and a *book* of remembrance was written before Him for those who fear the Lord . . ." It is also manifest by His *FUTURE* response (3:17-4:3)! In that future day of the Lord, He will honor the believing remnant: "*AND THEY WILL BE MINE,* says the Lord of hosts, *ON THAT DAY* that I prepare *MY OWN POSSESSION,* and I will SPARE THEM as a man spares his own son who serves him" (3:17). It is NOT VAIN TO SERVE THE LORD! The Lord sees our service; He remembers our labors. His reward may be *delayed* but it won't be denied. For the godless it will be denied. Thus, 4:1-3 speaks of the awful judgment awaiting those who have been superficial and external, but not genuine God-fearers.

C. THE CONCLUSION 4:4-6

The conclusion of the book of Malachi is both an admonition and a promise.

1.   THE ADMONITION 4:4

The people of Malachi's day are told to "REMEMBER THE LAW OF MOSES MY SERVANT, EVEN THE STATUTES AND ORDINANCES WHICH I COMMANDED HIM IN HOREB FOR ALL ISRAEL" (4:4). This is a warning needed by the majority of the nation, for they have been defying and neglecting the law and, thus, have been reaping chastisement.

2.   THE PROMISE 4:5-6

The promise looks forward: "BEHOLD, I AM GOING TO SEND YOU *ELIJAH THE PROPHET* BEFORE THE COMING OF THE GREAT AND TERRIBLE DAY OF THE LORD. AND HE WILL RESTORE THE HEARTS OF THE FATHERS TO THEIR CHILDREN, AND THE HEARTS OF THE CHILDREN TO THEIR FATHERS, LEST I COME AND SMITE THE LAND WITH A CURSE." This passage has always been a field for debate among Bible students. Let us note three views concerning the identification of *ELIJAH:*

a.   That this promise of the coming of Elijah was fulfilled entirely by *John the Bapist.*

b.   That Elijah will some day come *personally* and minister again.

c.   That one will come in the spirit and power of Elijah, but *not Elijah personally.*

This makes an interesting study in Scripture and your attention is directed to pp. 309–313 in "THINGS TO COME" by J. Dwight Pentecost where these three views are outlined and summarized. Scriptures that have to do with this are: Matthew 11:14; 17:10-13; Luke 1:17; John 1:21.

We have studied in general the twelve Minor Prophets. Merrill Unger says that "from Augustine's time (late 4th cen.), the Latin church has employed the term Minor Prophets because of their brevity (not their unimportance) as compared with the Major Prophets." Through our study of these twelve prophets we have confirmed that they are not of minor profit, but of great value for all Christians.